SOUNDS OF THE STRUGGLE:

Persons and Perspectives in Civil Rights

SOUNDS OF THE STRUGGLE:

Persons and Perspectives in Civil Rights

BY C. ERIC LINCOLN

William Morrow & Company, Inc.   New York

Apollo Edition 1968

Published simultaneously in Canada by George J. McLeod Limited, Toronto.

Printed in the United States of America.

Library of Congress Catalog Card Number 67-29822

TO JAY T. WRIGHT
Scholar, teacher, humanitarian

CONTENTS

CONTENTS

SOUNDS OF THE STRUGGLE:

Persons and Perspectives in Civil Rights

ANXIETY, FEAR, AND

INTEGRATION*

> O Rise! Shine! For the Light is a-coming . . .
> O Rise! Shine! For the Light is a-coming . . .
> O Rise! Shine! For the Light is a-coming . . .
> My Lord said he's coming bye-and-bye!
> This is the Year of Jubilee . . .
> (My Lord said He's coming bye-and-bye)
> My God has set his people free!
> (My Lord said He's coming bye-and-bye)
> Negro Spiritual

Mr. Justice Marshall, dissenting . . .

In respect of civil rights, common to all citizens, the Constitution of the United States does not, I think, permit any public authority to know the race of those entitled to be protected in the enjoyment of such rights. Every true man has pride of race, and under appropriate circumstances, when the rights of others, his equals before the law, are not to be affected, it is his privilege to express it as seems to him proper. . . . The thin disguise of "equal" accommodations . . . will not mislead anyone nor atone for the wrong this day done. . . ." [1]

Warren, C. J. . . .

We come then to the question presented: Does segregation of children in public schools solely on the basis of race, even

* Published in *Phylon*, 1960.

13

though the physical facilities and other "tangible" factors
may be equal, deprive the children of the minority group of
equal educational opportunities? We believe that it does.
. . . We conclude that in the field of public education the
doctrine of "separate but equal" has no place. Separate educational facilities are inherently unequal." [2]

FREEDOM, HISTORY, AND THE MORAL ORDER

History is always being redeemed, and man always has an
option to share in that redemption. The Civil War was fought
because intelligent men had transgressed the moral law and,
after a brief moment of repentance, set their teeth against it
in pursuit of a conflicting self-interest. Their self-interest was
not constructive, for despite the specious arguments of the
social Darwinists,[3] the racists,[4] and the Marxists alike, the
moral order interposes itself between man and the lower
species, and man, precisely because he is man, is not encom-
passed by any theorem that sacrifices the dignity of the person
to the survival of the "fit." On the human side of biological
existence, life may not, with impunity, feed on life.[5] There is
a quality inherent in human existence that sets human life
apart and makes it sacred. This is a fundamental law that has
informed every society in general, and *a fortiori*, every Christian society. History is redeemed, but it is not self-redemptive.
It is redeemed because human life is more than an incidental
quantity in the balance of nature. It has meaning and purpose.
But meaning is qualified, and purpose is negated wherever
freedom is not collateral to human existence. When one man
enslaves another, both men lose their freedom. Neither is, from
that point forward, available to participate in the common
ventures of life through which purpose is expressed and from
which meaning is derived.

The efforts of a society to exaggerate its own ego at the

expense of its moral values were foredoomed to failure, for values are ego-transcending. It is not incidental that the South displayed a marked ambivalence to the institution of slavery long before the Civil War brought it to an end. Washington had wished "to see some plan adopted by which slavery might be abolished by law"; and Patrick Henry, a distinguished fellow Virginian, concluded slavery to be "totally repugnant to the first impressions of right and wrong." Even Henry Clay, whose "practical" ambivalance about the matter finds its distressing counterpart in today's political *espieglerie*, found it profitable to announce, "If slavery be a blessing, the more of it the better and it is immaterial . . . whether the slaves be black or white . . ." [6] Indeed, they had been both black and white.[7] And red.[8] Clay's speech is the more dramatic because it was delivered in 1838, when the impending crisis made such sentiments hazardous. But such sentiments were by no means peculiar to politics, even among the South's greatest statesmen. The same spirit of moral truth that immortalized the Declaration of Independence through its recognitions of the self-evident quality of men had long before moved Thomas Jefferson to declare:

> The whole commerce between master and slave is a perpetual exercise of the most boisterous passions; . . . The man must be a prodigy who can retain his manners and morals undepraved by such circumstances. . . .[9]

By 1792 there was an abolition society in every state,[10] and of the dozens of such organizations that sprang up about the country in succeeding years, they remained concentrated in the South through the first quarter of the nineteenth century.[11] However, there was never a general sentiment for the discontinuance of slavery in the South, and in the heat of economic and political passions, which inflamed her as the mid-century approached, the South's moral leadership soon shriveled. With the invention of the cotton gin, the human chattels who were so lately lamented as economic liabilities [12] were suddenly conceived as the *sine qua non* of wealth and position.[13] Morality, as has so often been the case, capitulated to pressures and property. By 1840 the church could be indicted as the "Bulwark of American Slavery," and there were few who could challenge the allegation. Where Christianity might have led, in large measure it defaulted.[14]

The Civil War was fought. The issues which had refused to yield to reason and moral suasion were confirmed in blood and law. These issues were clear: ours was a

nation conceived in liberty and dedicated to the proposition that all men are created equal.[15]

This was no new truth. The principals reiterated by Mr. Lincoln were as old as human history. They are the fundamental principles of every charter of every true society, whether expressed or unexpressed. Indeed, except for the enhancement of liberty, and the security of equality, there can be no inducement for the formation of societies.[16] Whether "a nation so conceived and so dedicated" could endure was, and remains, academic. It is patent that no nation conceived in the *absence* of these principles can endure. Nor can any nation endure in which these principles are repressed.

But the war did not settle the issues. They remain to you and to me. Abraham Lincoln was under no illusions respecting the accomplishments of the war. The war had effected the physical liberty of the bondsmen, but it had not restored to prominence the lofty ideals of the great men who laid the foundations of this democracy. In a remarkable display of moral depth and social insight, Lincoln concluded his famous address at Gettysburg with this admonition:

It is for us the living rather to be dedicated here to the unfinished work which they who fought here have thus far so nobly advanced. *It is rather for us to be here dedicated to the great task remaining before us—that from these honored dead we take increased devotion* . . . that we here highly resolve that these dead shall not have died in vain, *that this nation under God shall have a new birth of freedom* . . . [The italics are mine.]

Current history in this, our homeland, would be considerably less embarrassed if Mr. Lincoln's counsel had been taken to heart. His apprehensions have proved to be prophetic. The adjustments we are now compelled to make could have been more easily managed at the close of the war. Men had died in order that the American creed might be restored to meaning. The way was clear for history to be redeemed, and man's opportunities for self-redemption through moral participation were fresh and disencumbered from the built-in restraints of local creed and traditions. The whole country, purged of the moral erosions that had qualified the faith which brought it into being, was now confronted with a challenge that is rare in history—a second chance to make its ideals come alive in less than a hundred years! That we failed then is evidenced by our present dilemma. Plessy vs. Ferguson has become the ignominious symbol of the lower values we chose in the face of more realistic possibilities.[17] "Separate" was never "equal," nor can it ever be by the very nature of the society of man and the dictates of the will of God.

Now, lacerated by a haunting anxiety, we are compelled to come to terms with destiny, a point on the perimeter of history that must inevitably level with the curbstone of truth.

THE ERA OF ANXIETY

Ours is an era that is characterized by fear and tension, loneliness and anxiety. Crime and delinquency, divorce and broken homes are no longer "statistics in the papers." They are real aspects of living for every American.[18] They are hazards we must presently accept as immediately relevant to each of us. There are no social islands; there is only the common main, and we are each a part of what happens to the rest. We are afraid. We are afraid of the future because we are haunted by the past. Our convictions echo their own emptiness, for they are devoid of courage and intention. For the most part, our convictions are for sale or exchange. Having been robbed of meaning, they are no longer dear. In our displaced conversation we say less and less about more and more, lest we uncover our anxieties and they betray our hidden selves.

> Our dried voices, when
> We whisper together,
> Are quiet and meaningless
> As wind in dry grass . . .[19]

We are preoccupied with inanities, lest somehow we be called to confront history come home to us.

Whatever the occasion for our anxieties, we cannot avoid encounter. If our apprehensions derive from the political stalemate with the Communist East, we must come to terms with this fact and seek new ways of resolution. If science has smashed our icons and robbed us of traditional securities, then an agonizing reappraisal of the source of our values and the *laws* of our security is indicated. If we, like most of the Western World, have had our moral slumbers suddenly and rudely disturbed by an unaccustomed tumult, we must arise forthwith and answer with integrity and responsibility.[20] *The clamor is for freedom.* Freedom and justice everywhere. In Budapest and in Birmingham. In Tibet and Tennessee. South Africa and South Carolina. Morocco and Mississippi.

Birmingham and Budapest represent essentially the same will to freedom on the one hand and the same rigid determination to maintain an anachronistic enslavement of human will and personality on the other. In Chicago as in the Congo, in Norfolk as in Natal, in Little Rock and Montgomery, those who fight for freedom and dignity, and those who destroy these values for all by denying them to some, are alike responding to a situation of anxiety. On the one hand, it is constructive normal anxiety that impels a people to creative self-affirmation, for normal anxiety, as Kierkegaard described it, involves "possibility—the possibility of freedom." [21] It is the anxiety that comes of not knowing the portent of history-to-be; yet it is the compelling inner necessity that determines a people to participate in that history as players and not as pawns. It is the constructive anxiety that man knows when he gazes into infinity—with awe and dismay—while he builds the rocket ship he hopes will take him there. Freedom is a possibility every man must plumb.

There is another kind of anxiety. It is the anxiety of violence and insecurity. It is the savage anxiety of the pogrom and the lynch mob. It is the anxiety of Warsaw and Poplarville, a pathological madness that deprives men of reason and reduces them to beasts. Rollo May calls such anxiety "neurotic," for it is entirely "disproportionate to the objective danger," and it diminishes an objective awareness of the situation as the situation in fact exists.[22] Its chief social manifestations have been the most extreme kind of antisocial behavior imaginable in modern civilization. Neurotic social anxiety derives from an unrealistic conflict within the "social person" that occurs whenever the will to freedom and creativity becomes the object of forces determined to repress these creative desires. It is significant that the moral, aesthetic, and intellectual values we claim as a highly literate and civilized people, the spiritual and religious principles we interpret as being the minimum demands of the responsible society, the common appreciation of fair play that structures our interpersonal relations, the political and judicial sanctions we so proudly hail as uniquely our own, all make for creativity, personal and social. But neurotic social anxiety arises and displays its characteristically irrational social violence whenever the society elects to forswear its creative responsibilities. A responsible society cannot ignore its social ulcers. Human life and human values collateral to life are involved. The wheel must turn. History has been lenient with us all, but after a time, even the gods grow weary.

"One of the marks of a responsible society is that the power to make decisions is widely distributed among the people." [23] If this is so, and I believe that it is, it seems to follow that social responsibility, which includes the responsibility to use this decision-making power in the common interest, is similarly distributed. Hence, no man can disclaim his share, for power and responsibility are collateral forces, and one does not occur in the absence of the other.[24] In this age of anxiety the most crucial decisions are indicated. With correct diagnosis, our anxieties and our fears may be conquered; with responsible commitment, we may restore to ourselves and to our fellows the dignity with which God endowed us all.

THE FEARS WE FACE

Anxiety is the basic reaction a man experiences with reference to what is perceived as a threat to his existence, or to the values he identifies with existence. It is an expression of man's awareness of his contingency, the possibility of being manipulated by forces not presently subject to his control. In its normal expression, anxiety is a condition of man's will to become himself, an expression of his freedom in the face of the unknown. It is the rejection of stasis at the beckon of possibility, and it confronts a perceived threat with a proportionate adjustment. Neurotic anxiety, on the other hand, represses and inhibits whatever demands creative expression, and it is characteristically disproportionate to the threat perceived.

Fear and anxiety are not interchangeable categories, for each of these reactions represents a threat to a different level of the personality. Anxiety is the reaction to an undifferentiated threat to one's total existence. It is a pervasive feeling of apprehension, a danger that is felt but unspecified. It is a haunting awareness that "all is not well" without knowing precisely why, or without knowing from what quarter the threat will materialize. If the threat is objectified, i.e., if the specific nature of the danger is recognized and its source is known, fear is the reaction indicated. Anxiety is the primal category; fear is a derivative reaction.[25] Anxiety is the response to a threat to the total existence; fear is a response to a threat that is less than ultimate. However, whenever the individual feels unable to cope with the specific dangers he perceives as threats, he may then regress into a situation of anxiety, that is, he will be threatened at the deeper level where life itself, or the set of values he considers necessary to living, is involved.

This is precisely what happens in a community or a nation where social change is either imminent or under way. A community may be considered to be a "social person," and it will exhibit in macrocosm many of the psychic phenomena of an individual person. Social anxiety, the anxiety of a community, is the collective anxiety of the people who compose that community. Similarly, social fear is the collective fear experienced by one social group when it conceives a different group as being a source of threat or danger. If the common consensus is that the threat may be successfully met and overcome through the instrumentality of some organized institution, such as the Army, or the local police department, or through the collective resources of the people, as for example "gentlemen's agreements" to restrict the sale of property to a particular

racial or religious group, then the threat is not experienced
below the level of fear. Similarly, if the perceived danger can
be "contained" by such social instruments as prisons, reservations, caste systems, traditions, religious taboos, and the like,
the threat does not strike at the "basic" level. It is when the
traditional defenses in a given society appear incapable of
either subduing or containing the perceived danger (e.g., the
struggle with communism) that social anxiety results, for the
threat is perceived as involving existence itself, or the values
identified with existence. We know in a general way that communism threatens us, or our "way of life," but we are uncertain as to when it will move in force against us or what form
its attack may take. Infiltration? Sabotage? Nuclear attack?
Is Soviet Russia the greater threat? Or Red China? Or will our
economic system with its spirals of inflation and periodic unemployment soften us up from within? If we could localize
the danger, we could contain it. Because we cannot, our
anxiety increases with each shift of foreign policy as we try
desperately to checkmate a danger that is both ubiquitous and
multiform.

To very many people the prospect of racial integration is
productive of an excruciating anxiety. When this anxiety is
widespread, or when it represents the general response in a
given community, it may be called "social anxiety." Every
anticipated social change is accompanied by an intensification
of anxiety factors, for change of whatever sort involves a relationship with the unknown or the unfamiliar. Where there
are different social groups involved, as in the present instance,
every group which is a party to the change will exhibit some
degree of anxiety in reference to it. Furthermore, the level of
anxiety will be affected by the following factors: (1) the rate
of the proposed change; (2) the anticipated degree of the
change; (3) the identity of the change agent; (4) the instrument of change; and (5) the social distance separating the

participants to the change. Thus the prospect of a sudden or very rapid change produces a more intense anxiety than does the expectation of a change that is to take place in the more distant future. This does not mean that the anxiety produced by the anticipation of an immediate change is more realistic, for where the implementation of social change has been both *sudden and resolute*,[26] the original intensification of social anxiety has usually subsided. On the other hand, if the change is projected too far into the future, it may become "lost" to present consciousness, reappearing as a "novel feature" with all of the terror of immediacy as the date of implementation suddenly approaches.

Similarly, the degree of change is likely to be more important in anticipation than in fact. What seems at the outset to be an impossible hurdle on confrontation turns out to be acceptable, or at least within the limits of toleration once it is a *fait accompli.*

The identity of the change agent and the instrument of change are related factors. A "respected" change agent with an effective instrument is the best combination for the reduction of anxiety. For example, a determined school board with efficient support from the municipal police department successfully reduced tension and anxiety during the integration of the Nashville schools. However, the instrument need not in every case be coercive. Love, religion, and the appeal to forgotten values may in some settings become as effective instruments for the reduction of anxiety as are court orders and civil penalties in others.

Social distance is perhaps the most important factor of all in social change involving racial integration, and social distance between Caucasians and Negroes is generally considered by the former to be polar. This concept of distance is especially pronounced in the South, precisely where the integration problem is presently centered.[27] Owing to the peculiar history of that region, the mere discussion of any change calculated to decrease this distance *in any degree* produces an amazing psychological distress on the part of the "social person" for which it has become a social shibboleth. Indeed, the whole pattern of race relations in the South has in the past been dictated ultimately in the interest of the preservation of this unique concept of social contraposition.[28] Americans have characteristically urged minorities to assimilate as rapidly as possible,[29] and once assimilation has taken place, an individual is expected to rise on his own merits to find his place in the social schema. This has always been an integral principle of the American creed. But in the case of Negroes, as with Chinese, Japanese and other nonwhites, race has precluded the possibility of assimilation, and assimilation is the narrow gate through which all must pass if social distance is to be reduced. Hence, Negroes, who are often most unlike whites in appearance, occupy a position conceived as farthest away from the social ideal, and this peculiar visibility of the Negro acts as a perpetual bar to the expression of any inherent faculties which might otherwise operate to close or narrow the social gap. So it is that any social change which threatens the barriers erected against social proximity is *a priori* conceived as a threat to the very core of the peculiar system of values so vital to the sense of security of a segregated community.

The anxiety evoked by the anticipation of social change is undifferentiated. If it is not resolved, it may well become *neurotic* and may consequently express itself in behavior that is irrational and disproportionate to the threat which excites it. The abandonment of public education in Little Rock and Virginia are examples of such behavior. The attempts on the life of a Negro student [30] who sought to attend the University of Alabama is a most extreme example, and it is indicative of the spirit-stripping [31] of which extreme anxiety is capable.[32] That it is also indicative of a displacement of moral values, and an unfortunate disregard for the principles of law and order, of course begs the question.[33] So long as the threat is undifferentiated, the affected community response is one of social anxiety. When the threat becomes objectified, i.e., is more precisely delineated, anxiety will be replaced by fear, except where the threat is conceived as envelopmental,[34] or where it is discovered to be of no dangerous consequence at all.

Fear is a response to a specific threat that does not involve existence or values held essential to existence. When, in the case of racial integration, anxiety is reduced to fear, progress may be made toward the effective resolution of the problems involved. But such progress is not automatic. A response of fear rather than one of anxiety does not mean that the change is either desired or that the opposing forces are even prepared to tolerate it. It may mean only that the *level of tension* is reduced because the perceived threat is no longer considered ultimate. "By reacting adequately to the various *specific* dangers which threaten him . . . the person avoids being threatened at the 'inner citadel' of his security system." [35] But fear, like anxiety, may be a response that is either positive or negative. In situations of social change, it may prompt constructive analysis of recognized problems with a view to their resolution (and the consequent elimination of the fear), or it may produce responses tending to strengthen the *status quo* or which may be otherwise designed to discourage change.

One of the most important problems confronting the parties involved in racial integration is how to reduce or eliminate social anxiety. This may be accomplished by (1) helping the white community understand that while there will be changes at certain levels of relationship, the entire *style of life* of the white community is not threatened; (2) by giving the Negro community concrete reason to believe that its *physical* life is not threatened. Implicit in these suggestions is the awareness that one element of the common community is concerned for its values; the other is concerned for its very existence. Reassurance is indicated in both instances if change is to take place with a minimum of tension and anxiety.

In terms of specific fears, the white man's anxiety derives from an understandable concern over such scarce values as jobs, social status, political participation, decent housing, education, and even religious affiliation. These are important values, but they are also universal in the sense that *every* American is presumed to both sanction and desire them and is by right of birth and citizenship eligible to compete for them. These are the common values of the democracy in which all of the people are entitled to share, except insofar as *individuals* may incur legal disqualification for such reasons as insanity or habitual criminality. But even such an *individual*, of whatever race, may not be arbitrarily excluded from his inherent right to participate in the normal benefits of his citizenship. Certainly racial preemption can never be a moral or legal condition of the availability or enjoyment of common opportunities for values held in common trust. We must now give serious consideration to the inherent unwholesomeness of a preemptive system of distribution in the midst of a Christian democracy. The white citizen is capable, I believe, of standing on his individual, intrinsic worth and so realizing his fair share of our common values. He does not need a set of racial crutches to maintain him in a situation of equality with reference to any racial minority. The American self-image is one of fair play; the American ideal is one of unqualified justice. A reexamination of both the image and the ideal seems indicated. The fear the white man knows respecting his nonwhite brother is a fear of fear itself, but it is productive of a burden of disabling consequences. We may no longer afford the doubtful luxury of compromising a common heritage of highest moral values in order that a more provincial and less inclusive code shall continue to operate to the advantage of some, while the legitimate claims of others are peremptorily denied. The moral order smiles on human aspiration; it is appalled by self-solicitude. As one American legal philosopher has put it:

> A responsible morals cannot be developed out of private mental states, subjective belief, or vaporous reveries. It requires a more social foundation.[36]

If white men are afraid of fear, Negroes are ofttimes afraid of freedom.[37] Freedom involves the confrontation of the unknown, the untried. It is a call to leave the familiarity of the usual for the possibilities inherent in what is unusual. It is the gadfly that perpetually worries the comfort of the sloth, no matter how degraded that comfort may be. Three hundred years of bondage and quasi-bondage have taken an understandable toll in constructive energy and self-respect. There are some who would swat the gadfly. . . .

That men shall be free is the irrepressible dictate of the moral law. Men *must* be free whether they will or not, for without freedom there is no responsibility, and responsibility is man's charter for participation in the historical process. Every man is endowed with an inalienable right:

> Life, liberty and the pursuit of happiness.

This, we are taught, is a self-evident truth. But if in America this escutcheon has been tarnished, whether through preemption or through disuse, there may yet be time to brighten it.

NOTES

[1] Quoted in Richard Hofstadter, *Great Issues in American History*, Vol. 2 (New York: Vintage, 1958), pp. 57, 58.

[2] *Ibid.*, pp. 59, 63.

[3] William G. Sumner, for example, who justified every kind of exploitation

in terms of an inevitable competition for survival. Said he, ". . . 'the strong' and 'the weak' are terms which admit of no definition unless they are made the equivalent to the industrious and the idle. . . . If we do not like the survival of the fittest, we have only one possible alternative, the survival of the unfittest. The former is the law of civilization; the latter is the law of anti-civilization." *Essays of William Graham Sumner,* ed. A. G. Keller and M. R. Devie (New Haven: Yale Press, 1934), Vol. 2, p. 56. See also Gordon Allport, *The Nature of Prejudice* (Garden City, N. Y.: Doubleday and Co., 1958), p. 106.

4 "Slavery was 'not a national evil' but, on the contrary, 'a national benefit,' a positive good, and one particularly appropriate for the Negroes as a group. . . . If there were sordid, servile and laborious tasks to be performed . . . was it not 'better that there should be sordid, servile and laborious beings to perform them?'" Quoted in Oscar Handlin, *Race and Nationality in American Life* (Garden City, N. Y.: Doubleday and Co., 1957), p. 32.

5 Marx, of course, would hardly grant "impunity" to the exploiting class. But his theory of class conflict denies man's intrinsic worth except as an economic factor.

6 Clay was highly controversial and rather contradictory. In a speech made before the House of Representatives (while he was Secretary of State) in 1827, he said of the free Negroes, "Of all classes of our population, the most vicious is that of the freed colored. It is the inevitable result of their moral, political and civil degradation." Benjamin Brawley, *A Social History of the American Negro* (New York: The Macmillan Co., 1921), pp. 125, 126. See also David Walker's indictment of Clay. *Ibid.,* pp. 155, 156.

7 See Handlin's discussion of "the Origins of Negro Slavery," *op. cit.*

8 *Ibid.*

9 Benjamin Brawley, *op. cit.,* p. 50.

10 *Ibid.,* p. 60.

11 *Ibid.,* p. 219.

12 Both Adam Smith and Benjamin Franklin had illustrated the relative expensiveness and wastefulness of slavery as an economic institution. Thackeray considered it "the dearest [i.e., costliest] institution that can be devised." "Of the 80 or 90 slaves on an average plantation," he said, "twenty are too sick or too old for work, . . . twenty too clumsy, twenty are too young, and have to be watched and nursed by ten more."

13 A hundred slaves for each 1,000 acres was the usual ratio for cotton farming. But the 100 able-bodied workers in the fields was exclusive of the aged, the young, and the specialists, mechanics and house servants left at home. J. C. Furnas in *Goodbye to Uncle Tom* (New York: William Sloane Associates, 1965), p. 113, estimates 250 as the average number of slaves actually involved in farming 1,000 acres of cotton. The market of slaves doubled within a few years after the new "gin" pushed cotton culture

westward into Alabama and Mississippi. So did the price (which fluctuated in Memphis and New Orleans with the cotton market). A healthy male slave who would have brought $400 in 1790 could easily be sold at $750 in 1845. By 1860 such a slave found a going market at $1500. In 1791 the United States exported 38 bales of cotton. In 1816 cotton worth $24,000,000 was exported, a figure greatly in excess of that approached by any other export. The moral fate of the South was sealed from then on.

[14] See Brawley, *op. cit.*, p. 219. The Methodist church is an interesting example. John Wesley had preached against slavery. In 1780 the Methodist Conference at Baltimore strongly condemned slavery, and in 1784 a slaveholder had been given the choice of repenting or leaving the conference. Yet by 1836 the church had suffered such a moral inversion as to be ready to disclaim "any right, wish, or intention to interfere in the civil and political relation between master and slave, as it existed in the slaveholding states of the Union."

[15] Abraham Lincoln's Gettysburg Address.

[16] Augustine demands, "Without justice, what are realms but great robber bonds?" C. H. McIllwain responds, "Justice and justice alone is the only possible bond that can unite men as a true *populus* in a real *res republica*." Quoted in Walter G. Muelder, *Foundations of the Responsible Society* (New York: Abingdon Press, 1959), p. 109.

[17] See Oscar Handlin, *op. cit.*, pp. 34 ff. Comments Prof. Handlin, "The destruction of slavery through the Civil War removed the ambiguities in the Negro's position. After emancipation, the law recognized no status but freedom . . . If the inferiority of the Negro was still to be asserted, it could not be on the basis of his race. The improvement in his position therefore proved temporary. The spread of racist ideas, unforeseen by the emancipators of 1865, soon consumed the fruits of liberation.

"The majority of the whites would under no circumstances yield their . . . superiority. To accept the equality of the Negro . . . would have amounted to an admission of guilt, not only for the injustices of slavery, but also for the disaster of the war. The inferiority of the Negro . . . was an article of faith made necessary by the society's history. . . .

"White superiority was now to be supported by a fixed pattern of relationships . . . The two groups were to remain apart and every contact—social, political, and economic—was to recognize and affirm the continuing inferiority of blacks to whites." Plessy vs. Ferguson gave these arrangements the sanction of law.

[18] Comments Rollo May, "we have become so inured to living in a state of quasi-anxiety, that our real danger is to hide our eyes in ostrich fashion." Rollo May, *Man's Search for Himself* (New York: W. W. Norton and Co., 1953), p. 35.

[19] From "We Are the Hollow Men," in *Collected Poems 1909–1962* by T. S. Eliot, copyright, 1936, by Harcourt, Brace & World, Inc.; copyright, © 1963, 1964, by T. S. Eliot. Reprinted by permission of the publishers.

[20] "It is neither God nor the physical universe the American fears . . . since he sees himself as the associate of one and the master of the other. What he truly fears in his fellowman." Francis L. K. Han, quoted by Selma C. Hirsh, *The Fears Men Live By* (New York: Harper and Bros., 1955), p. 3.

[21] "Freedom," says Rollo May, interpreting Kierkegaard, "is the goal of personality development. . . . The distinctive characteristic of man . . . lies in the range of man's possibility and in his awareness of his possibility. . . . Now this capacity for freedom brings with it anxiety . . . [which] is the state of man . . . when he confronts his freedom . . . Whenever possibility is visualized by an individual, anxiety is potentially present in the same experience." Rollo May, *The Meaning of Anxiety* (New York: The Ronald Press, 1950), pp. 32, 33.

[22] May believes that "neurotic anxiety . . . occurs when the incapacity for coping adequately with threats is not objective but subjective . . . [and] due to inner psychological patterns and conflicts. . . ." *Ibid.*

[23] Walter G. Muelder, *op. cit.*, p. 179.

[24] *Ibid.*, p. 108.

[25] May makes the following distinction: ". . . anxiety is the basic, under-lying reaction—the generic term—and fear is the expression of the same capacity in its specific, objectivated form." *Ibid.*, p. 205.

[26] As in the Armed Forces and certain situations of employment (e.g., sports), for example.

[27] See Arnold Rose, "Race, Beliefs and Facts," *The Negro in America* (New York: Harper, 1948), p. 31–54.

[28] *Ibid.*, "The Rank Order of Discriminations," p. 24. Also see Oscar Handlin, *op. cit.*, p. 36: "A comprehensive doctrine of race was essential to justify the developing patterns of segregation. The Negroes were a separate distinct biologically inferior species and that explained their degradation despite the futile effort to bestow freedom and equality upon them by law."

[29] See Arnold Rose's discussion of race and assimilation: "The Anti-Amalgamation Doctrine," *op. cit.*, pp. 21 f.

[30] Lucy, Autherine, 1956.

[31] Abandonment of spiritual values. Capitulation to provincial values when those values contradict previously held universal values.

[32] "Certainly . . . we may reflect that to call human sensuality and dissension 'bestial' insults the beasts. Man distends his lust and falls upon creatures of his own species with a fury of which no animal is capable." Paul Ramsey, *Basic Christian Ethics* (New York: Scribner's, 1954), p. 281.

[33] "The South is the only place in the world where one can get a reputation

for being a liberal simply by urging obedience to the law. . . ." Arnold Rose, *op. cit.*

[34] That is, where the sum total of available resources is conceived as inadequate to "subdue," "contain," or "avoid" the danger.

[35] Rollo May, *The Meaning of Anxiety*, p. 205.

[36] Edmond Cahn, *The Moral Decision* (Bloomington: Indiana University Press, 1955), p. 46.

[37] See Horace Cayton, "The Psychology of the Negro Under Discrimination," Arnold Rose, ed., *Race Prejudice and Discrimination* (New York: Alfred A. Knopf, 1953), pp. 276–90.

THE BLACK MUSLIMS

IN AMERICA*

The American conscience is like a Georgia mule drowsing under a mulberry tree: it will twitch where the fly bites, now here, now there, and so to sleep again.

This lethargy is the problem of America. She is neither more evil nor more immoral than any other nation, but she has a jaded social consciousness that has not been truly alerted since the time of the abolitionists. The 1954 school desegregation decisions and the student sit-ins have troubled her sleep, but they have not yet awakened her. She has not been stung in a tender enough spot in recent times. Perhaps the Black Muslims will find such a spot; if they do, and if they sting hard enough, we may all be benefited by the smarting.

The American Negro does not truly hate the white man. Not yet. For a long time Negroes have tried to convince themselves that the white man's resistance to social change derives not from a sense of racial superiority but from a twisted nationalism. Some Negroes, at least, are still willing to believe that the white man behaves as he does because he is American.

* Published in *Negro Digest*, June, 1961. Parts of this essay also appeared in C. Eric Lincoln's *The Black Muslims in America* (Boston: Beacon Press, 1961).

For most of us, there is no value quite so exalted as that implicit in being "American." All other values are subsidiary—religion, political affiliation, even moral consciousness. To be an American means to be associated with a great civilization, a unique civilization. We may share certain values with the rest of the world—values of religion and art, for example—but only we are Americans. We are the founders and developers of the heirs to the mightiest nation on earth, with a heritage unduplicated anywhere else in the world. But "American" also has an implication of color. Few of us have really lost the feeling that this is a "white man's country" and that all other races enjoy it by the white man's sufferance. We do not say this bluntly: it is considered in poor taste and, if quoted abroad, not in the national interest. But we act as if we were certain of its truth and validity. Our textbooks, mass media, and community behavior confirm this white nationalism everywhere.

A diminishing number of Negroes, therefore, believe that the Negro is rejected in America not primarily because of his race but because he is "not truly American." The Negro, they believe, is considered an alien, an outsider, for whom special adjustments must be made in law and custom. His color merely identifies him and serves to warn "real Americans" of his presence. The immediate result, of course, is the same: the Negro is barred from full participation in the values of citizenship. But the long-range prospect for a solution would be vastly different. If discrimination is based on pure racial antagonism, the white man will have to change his prejudice, for the Negro cannot change his skin. But if discrimination is based on national sentiment, the white man need not revise his thinking so drastically. He can still draw the comforting, sharp line between "American" and "not American"; he need only realize that his Negro neighbors are on the "American" side of the line. From there it would be a short step to accepting the Negro as an equal.

Sophistry? Perhaps—a sophistry encouraged by the Negro's desperate wish for a peaceful way out of his second-class prison. And like his more naïve, more pathetic trust in the white man's ultimate "good intentions," it has been all but completely shattered. A vestige of faith remains—but for how long? If the white man's conscience remains drugged, the flood of disillusion will soon sweep even this last frail hope away.

From time to time the trusting Negro has sought to prod the white man's moral sense indirectly—through the churches, the labor unions, and various interracial organizations—and by personal appeal. Always there has been a willingness to give the white man the benefit of every doubt. But nothing changed; and after a hundred years of waiting and hoping, the Negro finally went to court. Where he had been willing to accept "consideration," he now began demanding his rights —his rights to work, vote, buy a home, eat a meal, see a movie, worship in a church, ride a bus, sit in a public park, and send his children to school on the same terms as all of America's other first-class citizens. But the courts are slow, litigation is expensive, and the implementation of court rulings seems to be peculiarly uncertain in the area of civil rights.

So there has developed, in the last decade, a wide and dramatic spectrum of extralegal Negro protest. The passive Negro, who trusts that God and the NAACP will salvage his dignity while he concentrates on avoiding trouble, is rapidly becoming extinct. Those Negroes (most of them young) who still believe in the possibility of peaceful change have developed a bold but gentle technique to quicken the white man's conscience. They simply ignore restrictive laws and go wherever they know they have a moral right to be—on trains and buses, in restaurants and stores, public beaches and houses of God. These are not "angry young men"; they are not "bitter." They are just tired of waiting.

At the opposite end of the spectrum are the Black Muslims. They are angry; they are bitter; and they are also tired of waiting. Their response to white nationalism is extreme, and their militancy is barely restrained. But America can benefit from the lesson they seem intent upon teaching . . .

The Black Muslims are an intensely dedicated, tightly disciplined block of more than 100,000 American Negroes, convinced that they have learned the ultimate truth and ready to make any sacrifice it may demand of them. Theirs is not a "Sunday religion"; the Muslim temples hold frequent meetings, and every Muslim is required to attend two (and often more) meetings a week. Nor is it a religion that spares the billfold. The mass of Muslims are from the Negro lower class, with relatively low incomes, and they are encouraged to live respectably and provide for their families. But the men are urged to hold steady jobs; and all Muslims are forbidden to gamble, smoke, drink liquor, overeat, indulge in fripperies, or buy on credit. As a result most Muslims enjoy a healthy standard of living and still have enough cash left over to swell the movement's coffers.

Every Muslim is expected to give a fixed percentage of his income to the movement each year. In 1952 this percentage was set at one-third of all earnings; but the figure is probably not always so high. In addition, the temples collect contributions for a variety of funds, many for local purposes and at least six for the use of the national headquarters at Temple No. 2 in Chicago. Of the six known national funds, four are earmarked for real estate, public relations, official travel, and new cars; one is an annual collection on the anniversary of Prophet Wali Farad's birthday, February 26, with no purpose designated; and one is a discretionary fund, the "No. 2 Treasury and Central Point Fund," for Muhammad to use as he sees fit. The increase in the total funds available to the movement is suggested by the increase in its real estate holdings in

Chicago in the last six years—from an estimated $150,000 in 1954 to an estimated $500,000 at the end of 1960.

But the Muslims' power to influence the general American community is significant, not only because of their increasing membership and financial resources, but also because they can be mobilized to act in unswerving unison on any matter designated by the leadership. They will, for example, vote as Muhammad tells them to vote and buy where he tells them to buy. A Muslim bloc, therefore, even in a large city, may be the determining factor in the balance of political and economic power.

It is already said in Harlem that Malcolm X, minister of the large Temple No. 7 and Muhammad's chief lieutenant, is in a position to decide the election of U.S. Representative Adam Clayton Powell's successor, when and if Powell decides to retire. . . .[1]

Muhammad has not yet seen fit to use the undeniable power of the Black Muslim vote as a lever to prise concessions from the white or the non-Muslim Negro community. From the start, Muslims have generally preferred not to vote at all. This has been due partly to their self-identification with Afro-Asia, partly to their belief that America is already corrupt and doomed, and partly to their sense of futility in electing any white man to office. Malcolm X notes that "Roosevelt promised, Truman promised, Eisenhower promised. Negroes are still knocking on the door begging for civil rights . . . Do you mean to tell me that in a powerful country like this, a so-called Christian country, that a handful of men from the South can prevent the North, the West, the Central States and the East from giving Negroes the rights the Constitution says they already have? No! I don't believe that and neither do you. *No white man really wants the black man to have his rights, or*

[1] Malcolm X subsequently left the movement to found his own Organization of Afro-American Unity. He was assassinated February 21, 1965.

he'd have them! The United States does everything else it wants to do."

The Muslims have also refrained from voting in an effort to keep their strength a secret. "If you don't vote, nobody knows what you can accomplish when you do," and so far there has been no issue worth a real display of strength. In an address following the 1960 political conventions, Muhammad admonished some seven thousand Negroes at a New York meeting simply to "go to the polls with your eyes and ears open, and remember that it is not necessary for you to go seeking justice for anyone but yourselves. . . . The white people of America already have their freedom, justice and equal rights."

The time may come, however, when more than an undefined "justice" will be at stake. The Muslim leadership may one day feel ready to issue specific demands on local, state and national political bodies. Then, even at the national level, they can expect to be heard with respect. . . .

The Black Muslims' political power is ominous but, for the moment, latent. It is reckoned with seriously at the local and state level in many states, but Muhammad is not seeking political alignments even there, and he is unlikely to attempt a national power play for some years to come. The Muslims' economic power, on the other hand, is already being brought to bear against the white community. There is as yet no organized boycott of white merchants, but every Muslim is expected to "buy black"—that is, to trade with his own kind in preference to "spending your money where you can't work and can't sit down." Muslims have only contempt for the Negro sit-in movement, in which black men are "going out of their way to force the white man to let them spend more money with him" rather than contribute to the establishment of businesses run by and for black men.

The Muslims demand an entirely separate black economy,

arguing that not until the Negro is economically independent will he be, in any real sense, free. The total annual income of the American Negro, they point out, is more than $20 billion —greater than the total income of Canada and greater than that of several European states. Such a purchasing power, if spent among Negro businessmen and invested in Negro enterprises, would earn the respect of every nation in the world. The Muslims concede that the white man has, for the moment, an edge on technical and commercial know-how. The black man must learn whatever the white man can teach him and then outstrip the white man in productivity and trade.

As the Negro community develops its own business and industrial plant, the Muslims' pressure for economic separation is virtually certain to increase. In the not too distant future, this may well take the form of an official boycott against white merchants in the Negro ghettos. In a related move, the Muslims might picket the downtown stores so as to discourage Negroes from entering and shopping there. Such a maneuver would be so explosive that white store-owners and policemen might yearn for the good old days of the tension that accompanied the student sit-ins. Store-owners cannot be expected to take calmly the probable loss of much of their patronage; but the Muslims are neither "passive" nor "loving" toward white men, and any violence on the part of whites would certainly be met with violence. "If it ever happens," said one police official darkly, "that's when we're going to have hell on our hands."

THE BELIEVERS . . .

Who are these "faithful," these true believers, these Black Muslims?

Most simply, a Black Muslim is an American Negro who is a follower of Elijah Muhammad, "Spiritual Leader of the

Lost-Found Nation in the West." Black Muslims are distinguished from orthodox Moslems not in the mere spelling of the word (strictly speaking, either form is correct), but in their belief that their leader, the Honorable Elijah Muhammad, is the Messenger of Allah, directly commissioned by Allah himself, who came in person (under the name of Farad) to wake the sleeping black nation and rid them of the white man's age-old domination.

A survey taken in Detroit during the early years of the movement (1930–1934) showed that the overwhelming majority of Muslims—all but half a dozen or so of the two hundred families interviewed—were recent migrants from the rural South. The majority had come to industrial Detroit from small communities in Virginia, South Carolina, Georgia, Alabama, and Mississippi. Investigations by the Wayne County Prosecutor's office indicated the same origin.

Those attracted to the early movement were not only recent migrants, but they had typically visited their old homes in the South one or more times before becoming Muslims. The limited freedom they had experienced in the North made them acutely conscious of the extreme subordination of the Negro in the South—a realization which sharpened their hostilities and increased their sense of frustration.

In 1959 the pattern of membership remained generally the same, but the disproportion of recent, rural migrants did not appear so extreme. Several factors may be responsible. In the first place, the proportion of Negroes in the North and East is now much greater than it was in the depression years 1930–1934, and they have been there longer. The Muslims can thus proselytize a more established population. Secondly, although there is a continuing stream of migrants from the South, many of the current migrants are from Southern cities and towns, or at least have had some urban experience before pushing on to the North. The Black Muslim temples are scattered from

New England to San Diego and from San Francisco to Miami.
At least a dozen cities in the South have temples or missions. . . .

Critical observation and informal interviews have therefore
been the best tools available for determining the constituency
of the movement. My observations and experiences with Muslims in several cities suggest the following:

1. The membership is young. Up to 80 percent of a typical
congregation is between the ages of seventeen and thirty-five.
This pattern has been noted again and again in temples across
the country. In the newer temples, youth is even more pronounced; in some, fully three-quarters of the membership is
under thirty years of age. About the same proportion of the
ministers are under thirty-five; the youngest is only twenty-
three.

The reason for such a concentration of youth is clear. This
is an activist movement, and the appeal is directed to youth.
Large, young families are eagerly sought, and least attention
is paid to older people reared as Christians. Older people have
a certain security in their familiar religious orientation, and
they do not readily shift to a position so unfamiliar and radical
as that preached by the Muslims . . .

2. The membership is predominantly male. Unlike the typical Christian church, the Muslim temples attract many more
men than women, and men assume the full management of
temple affairs. Women are honored, and they perform important functions within a defined role; they are not in any
sense considered mere "property," as has sometimes been the
case in classical Islam. However, they do not constitute the
organizational foundation through which the movement functions, either in service or in finance. . . .

3. The membership is essentially lower class. . . . Recruit-
ment for the movement is still predominantly from among
low-income groups at the lower end of the educational scale.

It has attracted a few intellectuals, an increasing number of college students, and a scattering of business and professional men; but a majority of the membership of any given temple is composed of domestic and factory workers, common laborers, and the like. An increasing number of the men, however, are skilled and semiskilled craftsmen; the businesses owned by the group are usually housed in buildings renovated by the Muslims themselves—from the plumbing to the electric signs that mark the entrances. . . .

Many Muslims have come into the movement from various levels of extralegal activity. Some are ex-convicts—or even convicts, for at least three temples are behind prison walls. Some have come into the movement as dope addicts and alcoholics, or from careers as pimps and prostitutes, pool sharks and gamblers. But all who remain in the movement are rehabilitated and put to work. The members' claim that they are able to secure work much more easily than other Negroes appears valid. There are no idle Muslims; and delinquency, juvenile or adult, is almost unheard of.

Today's Muslims, however, do not generally live in the better residential areas available to Negroes. Where Negroes of middle- and upper-class status have developed—or moved into—residential areas consistent with their new prosperity, Muslims have not followed, for the movement continues to emphasize its affiliation with the working class. There are exceptions: Elijah Muhammad lives in a nineteen-room mansion in a quiet neighborhood near the University of Chicago. But the Messenger has an unusually large family (seven children); his offices occupy part of the building; and several rooms are set aside for the use of his many guests—ministers called to Chicago for consultation and, often, visitors from abroad. Even in this mansion there is no ostentation in furnishings or appointments, and few of Muhammad's ministers and followers have elected to abandon the slums.

The Muslim leaders tend to live and to build their temples and businesses in the areas from which they draw their major support—the heart of the Black Ghetto. . . .

4. The membership is almost wholly American Negro. The Garvey movement had been built around a hard core of West Indians, who, sharing Garvey's nationality and cultural experiences, were most readily attracted to his program. American Negroes gave Garvey little attention until he had already attracted a large following of West Indian immigrants. On the other hand, the Muslim leadership has not especially welcomed West Indian affiliation, possibly because the West Indian habit of making distinctions among Negroes in terms of color could jeopardize the Muslim appeal for a "United Black Front." . . .

5. Finally, the membership is predominantly ex-Christian. American Negroes have always been a religious people; and until very recent times, "religion" has for them meant Protestant Christianity. Except for the Moorish-Americans and a few hundred ex-cultists of varying past proclivities, almost all of the Muslims seem to be drawn from Protestant families or traditions, although there are significant numbers of ex-Catholics in the movement. Many Muslims have come from revivalistic sects, but a substantial number have held active membership in the established denominations, and some of the Muslim ministers are former Christian preachers.

The younger Muslims, especially those under twenty, have usually had no strong Christian convictions, but almost without exception they come from Christian homes. All too often their conversation reflects a serious inadequacy in their religious environment. One parent whose son had "gone Muslim" turned to his minister in anguish. "Now," said the minister, "he expects me to save his son from the Muslims when I haven't a single handle to grab him by. The parents come here four or five times a year, and the boy doesn't come at all. No wonder the Muslims got him; he was looking for something."

. . . AND WHY THEY BECOME BELIEVERS

The fundamental attraction of the Black Muslim movement is its passion for group solidarity, its exaggerated sense of consciousness-of-kind. What matters above all is that men acknowledge themselves as black or white, and that all black men work together to accomplish their group aims. These aims have been summed up by a Muslim minister as:

To get the white man's foot off my neck, his hand out of my pocket, and his carcass off my back. To sleep in my own bed without fear, and to look straight into his cold blue eyes and call him a liar every time he parts his lips.

The ultimate appeal of the movement, therefore, is the chance to become identified with a power strong enough to overcome the domination of the white man—and perhaps even to subordinate him in turn.

In this context, although the Black Muslims call their movement a religion, religious values are of secondary importance. They are not part of the movement's basic appeal, except to the extent that they foster and strengthen the sense of group solidarity.

The Muslims make no secret of the fact that they count themselves a part of the growing alliance of nonwhite peoples, which they expect eventually to inundate the white race, washing away the hated supremacy that that race has so long enjoyed. Almost fifteen years ago Dr. Buell Gallagher warned about orthodox Islam:

There are signs that the Pan-Islamic movement may harden into a new political nationalism, based on race, which may replace the Islam of an international and interracial brother-

hood. This Pan-Islamic spirit which appears about to come to
full fruition in a union of the entire Muslim world against the
rest of the globe is one of tomorrow's imponderables. . . .[2]

Gallagher did not refer to, or even contemplate, the Black
Muslims, yet his words are pertinent to them. The Muslims
are not recognized by orthodox Moslems in this country, but
they consider themselves Moslems and are apparently so considered by the many Moslem countries in Africa and the
Middle East who have welcomed and honored their leaders.
Certainly, to the extent that the Pan-Islamic goal is a power
structure forged out of anti-white sentiment, these goals are
shared by the Black Muslims in America.

The anti-Christian tone of much of the Muslim teaching
also has a strong attraction for some Negroes. Occasionally
this attraction is personal, as with the youth rebelling against
a parental authority which has been symbolized by enforced
church attendance. But increasing numbers of Negroes are
disillusioned by the continuation of racial segregation in the
church and are coming to identify the church with social
apathy and racial subordination. To these disaffected Christians the Muslims make a shrewd appeal. On the one hand,
aware that the Christian tradition rejects hatred, they proclaim
a positive slogan: "Not anti-white, just pro-black. We're so
pro-black we haven't time to be anti anything." But at the
same time they insist on the close link between the Christian
church and white supremacy. . . .

Because Christianity is "the white man's religion," the repudiation of Christianity is an overt act of aggression against
the white man. To be identified with a movement that openly
rejects the fundamental values of the powerful majority is to
increase vastly one's self-esteem and one's stature among one's
peers. . . .

[2] *Color and Conscience* (New York: Harper and Brothers, 1946), p. 191.

The challenge of an ascetic ideal, balanced by the absence of social barriers to affiliation and service, has brought thousands under the banner of Muhammad. Probably in no other religious organization are alcoholics, ex-convicts, pimps, prostitutes, and narcotic addicts welcomed so sincerely. The Christian church is, in most instances, careful to take none to its bosom until they are cleansed. The Muslims welcome the most unregenerate and then set about to rehabilitate them. They have stern rules of conduct, but no man is condemned for what he was—only for what he refuses to be. . . .

The stress upon—and the outward manifestation of—fraternal responsibility is a strong attraction for many Negroes, whose social and civil insecurity is often extreme. The Negro has often been characterized as a ready "joiner," and more often than not this characterization has been justified. He is compelled to join in order to escape the isolation and sense of helplessness he experiences as a social outcast. He joins for recreation (when public recreation is not available to him) and for security against sickness and want. He joins for consolation and companionship—the attempt at flight of an earthbound Negro in a white man's world.

All these elements are present, to some degree, in the appeal of Muslim membership. But the appeal goes deeper: every Muslim holds himself ready to die for his brother, and more especially for his sister. This extreme solidarity attracts not only those in search of security but also those in search of a cause—a focus for the free-floating hostility that racial oppression always breeds. In 1958 a Muslim was arrested in New York City (on a false identification, as it turned out). Within an hour, several hundred of his brothers turned up at the precinct station in a quiet show of fraternal solidarity to insist that "justice be done." They waited patiently and quietly until the wrongly accused man was released; then they took him away with them. Membership in the local temple immediately spiraled. Their show of solidarity had won what the Negro community interpreted as an important victory.

The intensity of this sense of unity makes unnecessary the usual trappings of organizations which emphasize group solidarity. It is unrealistic (though at least one Negro leader has done so) to dismiss the movement as "another mutual admiration cult—another opportunity for people who aren't going anywhere to hang out the signs to prove it." The usual "signs" of social status associated with Negro organizations are fanciful titles and flamboyant uniforms. Among the Black Muslims, however, there are no phony "doctors" or specious "saints," no uniforms and no prestige offices. The only titles are those given to Muhammad and to the hierarchy of the secret military organization, the Fruit of Islam. To be called a "brother" or a "sister" is the highest compliment a Muslim can be paid, for (as Minister Louis X of Boston puts it) "we were brothers before we were ministers." Christians, of course, also call each other "brother" and "sister" at times, but one senses that the Muslims are appealing to something beyond ordinary religious courtesy.

Another aspect of the movement that has strong appeal-value is its emphasis upon youth and masculinity. The ministers are young and personable; some have been entertainers or have otherwise had public followings. All Muslim men are clean-shaven, close-cropped, and well-dressed in conservative clothes whenever they appear in public. Inside the temples there is a constant movement of young men with military bearing; they move quietly but with an unexaggerated dignity and the inescapable suggestion of latent force. They wear no uniforms or insignia except for a small star-and-crescent button in their lapels. Polite and self-assured, they seem alert to the demands of the present and confident of the future. Their attitude toward Christian Negroes is not quite one of condescension, nor yet one of toleration. It is more a kind of patient amazement that intelligent people could be unimpressed with the Messenger's dicta or could still find it possible to want to live in the world of the white man.

These are the "Young Blacks" who will usher in the Black Nation of Islam. "We are not looking for crumbs," says Malcolm X.

In America today, where the so-called Negro is concerned, you have a high degree of dissatisfaction. It is hard for me to believe that the white man, as intelligent as he is, cannot realize the degree of dissatisfaction in the minds of the young generation of black men. The old generation forgets . . . It is on its way out . . . What you [whites] have to know now is what the black man is thinking [whom] you will have to deal with in the future.[3]

A surprising number of young people are attracted by the Muslim's redefinition of the roles men and women should play in the home and in the religious life of the sect. There is a strong emphasis on the equality of individuals irrespective of sex, but each sex is assigned a role considered proper to itself. The trend in our larger society today seems to be toward blurring the distinct line between the traditional social roles of men and women. The Muslims, on the other hand, claim to have restored the woman to a place of dignity and respect, while restoring to the man his traditional responsibilities as head of the family. Muslim women seem to welcome the security and protection implicit in this arrangement, and the men seem to exhibit a deeper sense of responsibility than is common to others of the working class. Children seem to profit the most, for among Muslim children, delinquency is almost unheard of.

Finally, the Negro-oriented parochial schools maintained

[3] Malcolm X at Boston University Human Relations Center, February 15, 1960.

by the Muslims in Detroit and Chicago have attracted some followers. If, as is planned, the Muslims establish schools in most of the larger cities where they have temples, their numbers will probably increase proportionately. One Chicago domestic, who was not a Muslim, was asked whether she sent her children to the Muslim school in her neighborhood. "Well, no, sir," she replied with some hesitation. "But my husband, he's been talking about it. Whatever he says. They teach the children how to behave up there, and they teach them something about ourselves, too—all about what the colored people have done in the world, not just the white. You ought to know something about your own people, don't you think? Especially if you're going to live in a free country."

Few if any children of the middle- or upper-class Negro families attend the Muslim schools, for not many of their parents are in the movement. Yet there is a widespread sympathy for the Muslim curriculum emphasis on the history of the Negro in America and on the black African civilizations of the pre-Colonial era. This is often expressed obliquely by resentment of the completely white-oriented training given to almost all Negro children. Said one Nashville intellectual: "They grow up, and they don't know who the hell they are. They aren't white, and white rejects them. But white is all they know about. And you talk about adjustment! It's a wonder any of us survive!" . . .

The Black Muslims are not an isolated phenomenon. They are rooted in the whole structure of racial tension. In New York City alone, a score of more organizations operate in the name of black solidarity. Their central theme is always the glorification of black civilization and the deprecation of the white man's culture, which, whenever it has been adopted by the black man, has reduced him to impotence and ignominy.

In the South, where resentment of the white man has until recently been less overt, black nationalism has expressed itself in lodges and fraternal societies, in which tens of thousands of Negroes learn various "ancient rites" of supposed Afro-Asian origin. Every Negro community in the South has its multitude of legends illustrating the Negro's superior physical strength, sexual prowess, and moral integrity. "Mr. Charlie" is never a match for the cunning of "Ol' John." And "Miss Ann," though she is "as good a ol' white woman" as can be found anywhere, remains in the mind of the Southern Negro a *white* woman and, therefore, a legitimate target for the petty machinations of her Negro servant, "Annie Mae."

Most Negroes do not, of course, spend most of their time "thinking black." But no part of Negro life is wholly free of this glorification. A defensive kind of black nationalism finds occasional expression in the quarrels of Negro children everywhere. "Black is honest," they cry out, and the "blacker the berry, the sweeter the juice." Even the Negro churches are often tinged with nationalism. An obscure African slave who rescued the prophet Jeremiah from a cistern into which he had been thrown by his enemies is exalted as a symbol of righteousness and fearlessness in the service of God. It has also been interpreted as the symbolic rescue of the Jews by the black man.

From the soil of repression and hostility grow bitter fruits, and black nationalism is one of the most bitter. It feeds on the prejudices, stereotypes, and discriminations which tend to characterize relations between whites and blacks in America. It accepts the white man's allegation that there are "inherent differences" between people who have different colored skins. But it inverts the values: it worships what it cannot change. It forges a weapon of vengeance for the black man out of the very attributes for which he is held to be inferior.

The Black Muslims have made a science of black nationalism. They have made black the ideal, the ultimate value; they have proclaimed the black man to be the primogenitor of all civilization, the Chosen of Allah, "the rightful ruler of the Planet Earth." And their extreme racist doctrine has attracted more than a hundred thousand adherents—a vivid warning of the deep resentment American Negroes harbor for their status in our society and of the futility they feel about the likelihood of a genuine and peaceful change.

THE BLACK MUSLIMS*

The Black Muslim movement had its beginning in the black ghetto of Detroit. The time was 1930. It was the first year of the great depression, an era of hunger, confusion, disillusionment, despair, and discontent, a period of widespread fear and anxiety. Between 1900 and 1930, two and a quarter million Negroes left the farms and plantations of the South. Most of them migrated to selected urban areas of the North—New York, Philadelphia, Chicago, and Detroit were among the most popular destinations. The Negro population of Detroit increased 611 per cent during the ten years from 1910 to 1920. During the same period the total Negro population in the North soared from a mere 75,000 to 300,000, an increase of 400 per cent.

Floods, crop failures, boll weevils, and night-raiding Klansmen all served to hasten the Negro's exodus from the South. One hundred Negroes were lynched during the first year of the twentieth century. By the outbreak of World War I in 1914, the number lynched stood at 1,100. When the war was over, the practice was resumed—twenty-eight Negroes were burned alive between 1918 and 1921. Scores of others were dispatched by equally cruel methods.

* Published in *The Progressive*, December, 1962.

The Negroes who left the South were temporarily welcomed in the North, although the congenialities of the North have always been of an impersonal sort. Many industries sent agents into the South to lure the Negroes north with promises of good jobs, but the Negro was soon to find that it was only his labor and not his presence that was wanted.

After the war was over, the Negroes' welcome in the North wore thin. They found it increasingly hard to get jobs except as strikebreakers, for there were no longer enough jobs to go around. Thousands of Negroes were fired and replaced with white men. There was not enough housing, and Negroes were crowded into the infamous black ghettos in the most deteriorated part of the inner city. Landlords and law-enforcement agencies alike were unsympathetic. But still the Negroes came out of the South. Few had skills; many were illiterate; all were filled with hope for something better than they had left. Soon there were hunger and crime and delinquency—and police brutality. The bright promise of the North had failed. Hope turned to desperation.

It is an interesting historical phenomenon that when a people reach the precipice of despair, there is so often waiting in the bushes a savior—a messiah who promises to snatch them back from the edge of the abyss and turn their grief into greatness. So it was in Detroit. There appeared in the black ghetto a mysterious Mullah who called himself W. D. Farad Muhammad. He had come, he told the handful of Negroes who gathered to hear him, from the Holy City of Mecca. His mission was "to wake the 'Dead Nation in the West'; to teach them the truth about the white man, and to prepare them for the Armageddon." The Armageddon? What did this apocalyptic concept have to do with the problems of the Negro in America? Farad was explicit on this point: In the Book of Revelation it is promised that there must be a final battle between good and evil, and it is to take place at Armageddon, "the

Mountain of Megiddo," in the Great Plain of Esdraelon in Asia Minor. But the Bible has a cryptic message for the initiated of Black Islam: The forces of "good and evil" are the forces of "black and white." "The Valley of Esdraelon" symbolizes the "Wilderness of North America." The battle of Armageddon is to be the black man's final confrontation of the race which has so long oppressed him.

At first Farad, who was at the time thought to be a Prophet (but who after his departure was recognized as Allah himself), met from house to house with small groups of Negroes. He went about his mission as unobtrusively as possible, listening to the problems of destitute Negroes, sharing whatever they had to offer him. A contemporary who later heeded the muezzin's call recalls his *modus operandi* as that of a salesman who "came first to our house selling raincoats, and afterwards, silks. In this way," the convert said, "he could get into the people's houses. . . . If we asked him to eat with us, he would eat whatever we had on the table, but after the meal he began to talk. . . ." [1]

The fame of the Prophet spread, and he soon established the first of the Temples of Islam in Detroit. As his following increased, Farad grew more bold in his attacks upon the habits and the culture symbols the Negroes had always taken for granted. He taught the new Muslims that they were not Negroes, but "black men." The word "Negro" was an invention of the white man designed better to identify his victims and separate them from their Asian and African brothers, he said. Further, the so-called Negro was not an American, but an "Asiatic," for his forefathers had been stolen from the Afro-Asian continent by the white slavemasters who came there in the name of Jesus with a Bible in one hand and a set of manacles in the other. Christianity, the Prophet taught, was a white

[1] Quoted in *The Black Muslims in America, op. cit.*, p. 10.

man's religion, a contrivance designed solely for the enslavement of nonwhite peoples like themselves. Wherever Christianity has gone, he declared, men have lost their liberty and their freedom. Islam was declared to be "the natural religion of the black man." Only in Islam could the so-called Negroes find freedom, justice, and equality.

Little by little the Prophet began to enlighten these disillusioned migrants from the South about their true history and their place in the future. Black man was the original man, he taught. On the continent of Afro-Asia "black civilizations flourished long before the white man stood up on his hind legs and crept out of the caves of Europe." Further, the Prophet said, the white man is a devil by nature; he is the physical embodiment of the principle of evil, and he is incapable of doing good. "He is," said Farad, "the eternal adversary of the one true God whose right and proper name is Allah."

By "tricknology" the blue-eyed devils had enslaved the black man, Allah's chosen people. They had taken away their native language (which was Arabic) and forced them to speak English, a foreign tongue. The white man had taken away their names, i.e., their identity, and given them European names, which every black man should hate as badges of slavery. Above all, the cruel slavemaster took away their natural religion and made them worship a blue-eyed Jesus with blond hair, telling them that this was their God.

The so-called Negroes, who, unknown to themselves, comprised "The Nation of Islam in the West," had been brainwashed and given a false image of themselves by their white teachers. They had been lulled into submission by the white Christian preachers who promised them a home "over Jordan" when they could no longer hew the wood and draw the water for the white man's comfort.

The wheel must turn, the Prophet insisted. The nation of Islam has a manifest destiny. Armageddon must come. It will come as soon as the black man in America learns who he is and accepts the truth about the white man the Prophet was sent to declare.

Not all of Farad's energies were spent in attacking the white man. He taught his followers cleanliness and thrift. He persuaded them to give up liquor and such "unclean" foods as pork, corn bread, peas, possums, and catfish, bidding them to separate themselves from the habits they had acquired in slavery. He established a school where homemaking, Negro history, Arabic, and other subjects of interest to the Muslims were taught. He demanded that his followers be clean at all times, bathing at least once a day. He taught them to give an honest day's work for an honest day's pay, to be respectful to others, and, above all, to respect themselves. They must obey "all constituted authority," but they must require of their adversaries "an eye for an eye and a tooth for a tooth."

The Prophet's first appearance in Detroit is dated as July 4, 1930, and no one can remember seeing him after June 30, 1934. There are many legends but no authentic information as to where he went. But four years of preaching left some 8,000 Black Muslims with a new self-image based on a counter-myth of black superiority.

However, the Prophet had not left himself without a witness. Early in his brief ministry in Detroit he had attracted the admiration and loyalty of a young Negro from the town of Sandersville, Georgia—Elijah Poole, son of a Baptist minister. Poole, already embittered by the harshness of race relations in the South, had migrated to Detroit with his family in the early 1920's. His disillusionment with the "promised land" was immediate, for he soon discovered that the limitations which prescribed his place in the North differed only in degree from the familiar pattern of circumscription in the South. For a time better jobs were available in the North, but Poole was soon to discover that job security operated on a racial basis. Housing was more strictly segregated than in the South, and living conditions in the black ghetto were often worse than they had been in the sharecroppers' cabins. The lynchings in the South had their counterparts in the race riots of the North. And everywhere police brutality was the same.

The belittling paternalism of the South had been replaced by the cold indifference of the North, and Elijah Poole found himself and his family with no better chance of assimilation in the great "melting pot" of the North than he had known in Georgia. Poole's contact with foreign-born elements speaking in strange "un-American" accents and wearing "foreign" clothes increased his feelings of isolation and frustration. He saw the Negroes' jobs taken from them and given to white men who had not fought for this country, and who in some cases had fought against it; and he was embittered by the creeping realization that, in the North as in the South, the color of a man's skin, not the order of his citizenship or the quality of his intrinsic worth, was the determining factor in all his important social relationships.

Elijah was ready for the racist doctrines of Wali Farad, and from their first meeting he became the Prophet's most dedicated aspostle and his chief amanuensis. Farad had identified the black man's oppressor in terms never before heard in the Negro community. He had exposed the white man as a devil —a literal devil, created on the Isle of Patmos by a madman whose name was Yakub. This was the secret of the white man's power, his cruelty, and his vulnerability. Allah had given the white devils a certain time to rule, and the time was up. The black man must prepare himself for the Armageddon.

To Elijah Poole, Farad entrusted his mantle and his mission. He made Poole First Minister of Islam and put the Muslim school, the training of the ministers, and the highly secret Fruit of Islam (the FOI is the leadership training corps for the Armageddon) under his direction. Later, Poole was sent to

Chicago to found Temple No. 2, the present headquarters of the movement.

In recognition of Poole's dedicated and effective leadership, Farad relieved him of his "slave name," Poole, and honored him with the Muslim name, "Muhammad." Thereafter Farad's public appearances were progressively less frequent until the day of his final disappearance.

Under Elijah Muhammad the movement has spread from the initial temple in Detroit to almost every major city in the country with a sizable Negro population. In most of these cities there is a temple. In others where the movement is more inchoate, there are missions. Where there are no missions there are likely to be representatives of the movement who are in touch with the Muslim leadership in nearby cities.

There are Muslim units in many of the state and federal prisons across the country, for the movement finds its prison audiences to be ready-made and highly receptive. Here the racial character of most law-enforcement agencies, courts, and custodial personnel is an important factor in sharpening the prisoner's resentments and his sense of persecution.

The Black Muslims are among the best organized and most articulate of the protest movements. In terms of their immediate internal objectives, they have a highly effective leadership, some of which has been recruited from the Christian churches and retrained by Elijah Muhammad to serve the cause of Black Islam. Their newspapers and magazines are superior in layout and technical quality to much of the Negro press; and the financial support of the movement is probably higher in proportion to income than that of most similar organizations. Yet the Black Muslims are not generally acceptable to the spirit of protest which has won universal respect and frequent admiration for other Negro protest organizations.

Generally speaking, the movement has been a protest directed at the whole structure of the white Christian society, a society to which the Black Muslims feel themselves (as Negroes) to be an isolated and unappreciated appendage. Hence, the burden of their protest is against their retention in a society where they are not wanted. They clamor for some land of their own—"some of this good earth" on which to establish their own black nation. This is the soft side of the Armageddon complex which looks to the removal of the white devils as the source of their discomfiture rather than to going anywhere themselves. Elijah Muhammad teaches that "the white man's home is in Europe" and that "there will be no peace until every man is in his own country."

In a recent issue of the official Muslim newspaper, *Mr. Muhammad Speaks*, the Muslims stated their protests in the form of ten propositions demanding "full and complete freedom, equal justice under the law, and equality of opportunity." They further demanded that as the descendants of slaves who had contributed so much to the making of America without compensation, they should be given a separate territory— "fertile and minerally rich"—which should be subsidized by the federal government "for the next twenty to twenty-five years" until the black nation is able to produce for its own needs.

The Muslims say they see no audaciousness in such a proposal "inasmuch as the federal government is presently underwriting the economies of half the nations of the world, many of which are Communist, and others which accept our money and then tell us 'go home.' " "We believe," says Minister Malcolm X, "that the so-called Negroes who have been more loyal to America than any other ethnic group, and who served America for three hundred years in absolute slavery, and another hundred years since the Civil War in semislavery, have a right to expect something for their labor. If we can pay the Indians for the land stolen from their forefathers, we can pay the so-called Negroes for the exploited lives of their ancestors who served in slavery. Life is worth more than land."

The Muslims also say they want "freedom for all believers now held in federal prison . . . and freedom for all black men and women now held under death sentence in innumerable prisons in the North as well as in the South." They demand "an immediate end to police brutality and mob attacks against Negroes throughout the United States," and they want the federal government to "intercede to see that black men and women tried in which courts secure justice in accordance with the laws of the land." [2] If the government is unwilling or unable to do this, the Muslims argue, then they want the government to "allow them to build a new nation for themselves dedicated to justice, freedom, and liberty."

Finally, until they are given a separate territory for their black nation, Muhammad charges that the least the government can do is to provide immediate equal employment opportunities for its "so-called Negroes, and exempt them from all taxation as long as they are deprived of equal justice." As a sort of postscript to his catalogue of political and economic demands, the Muslim minister wants Negro children to have "equal education" (in schools segregated by sex), and he wants "all black children taught and trained by their own black teacher." Intermarriage must be strictly prohibited and "the religion of Islam taught without hindrance or suppression."

Taken at face value, and with quite obvious exceptions, the protests and demands of the Black Muslims as stated do not seem unreasonable. I do not know any Americans who do not want freedom. Justice under the law, equality of opportunity, and freedom of worship are all approved values in our society, and they find their sanctions in the American creed. Further,

[2] "The Muslim Program," *Muhammad Speaks*, March 4, 1966.

they are objectives which are implicit in the programs of all other Negro protest movements. But there are other factors which qualify the Muslim protest movement and make it unacceptable to the general American public.

The Muslims have abandoned the fundamental principles of the American creed as having no practical relevance to them or their conditions of existence. They have substituted in its place a new system of values perceived as more consistent with the realities of their peculiar circumstances. This is a unique departure by an organized group in American history. No other racial or ethnic group has so deliberately and so completely rejected the fundamental premises or values implicit in the American creed. The Black Muslims quite properly identify these values with white Christian culture, and in their resentment of their subordinated status in a white-oriented society, they reject not only the symbols of subordination but the very principles which, though imperfectly expressed in practice, provide the ideal goals which order our social behavior.

I am not saying that the Muslims are "un-American," for the American creed is not a legal or constitutional document against which the political loyalty of a group may be measured. Rather, it is a common set of beliefs and values in which Americans have nominally found consensus. It is a body of ideals, a social philosophy which affirms the basic dignity of every individual and the existence of certain inalienable rights without respect to race, creed, or color.

By the nature of certain of their goals and requirements, the Black Muslims have exempted themselves from the aegis of the American creed. In their ardent racism and their insistence upon physical and political separation in a black nation of their own, in their repudiation of American citizenship, they exclude themselves from principles and values which have not functioned to secure to them the rights and privileges they feel to be consistent with human dignity.

Other groups advocate *white* supremacy, resist the assimilation of Negroes and others, and practice hatred rather than love. Yet they remain "loyal" to the American creed. Why single out the Muslims as beyond the pale? The point is that although the creed is violated constantly in practice, it remains an *ideal* to which most other organizations of questionable dedication—not excluding the Klan, the White Citizens Councils, and the John Birch Society—give their assent; an ideal in which they allegedly derive their interpretations of moral values and social justice.

The Black Muslim movement is not so much a violation of the American creed as it is the substitution of new principles and new values which are antithetical to it. The movement has in effect promulgated a *new* creed based on a radically different interpretation of history, promising a new order which will insure a reversal of the black man's status in relation to the hated white devils.

Black Muslims do not "just happen." They are symbols of our failure to meet effectively the minimum needs of large numbers of human beings who, deprived of traditional incentives and realistic participation in the common values of our society, are looking for a cause and a leader. They are the victims of neurotic social anxiety, people who are repeatedly frustrated in their attempts to make adjustments in a society which is unaware of their existence except as the faceless subjects of statistical data. The future of the Black Muslim movement is hard to predict. But whatever that future may be, we shall all be in part responsible.

EXTREMIST ATTITUDES IN

THE BLACK MUSLIM MOVEMENT*

On Sunday, the third of June, a hundred and thirty white persons met their deaths in an airplane crash outside of Paris, France. All but ten of the victims were from Atlanta, Georgia.

When news of the tragedy was received in this country the typical American experienced some sense of loss and identification with the bereaved relatives and friends of those who perished. In Atlanta, as the news came in over the radio, church services were interrupted to offer special prayers for the repose of the dead and the comfort of their survivors.

No members of any of the families of any of the victims of the crash were worshiping in any Negro churches in Atlanta, for the churches in that city are segregated. But in the Negro churches, too, services were interrupted and prayers were said on behalf of the dead and bereaved.

In a Los Angeles church the announcement of the plane crash was received as a beatific revelation of the avenging spirit of Allah. Minister Malcolm X, peripatetic internuncio of the Black Muslim movement, interrupted his recitation of the white man's abuses against nonwhite Americans to share the good news with some 1,500 Negroes who had gathered to hear him:

* Published in *New South*, January, 1963.

"I would like to announce a very beautiful thing that has happened. . . . I got a wire from God today [laughter]. Wait, all right, well, somebody came and told me that he really had answered our prayers in France.

"He dropped an airplane out of the sky with over one hundred and twenty white people on [*sic*] it because the Muslims believe in an eye for an eye and a tooth for a tooth. But thanks to God, or Jehovah or Allah, we will continue to pray and we hope that every day another plane falls out of the sky.

"We call on our God—He gets rid of one hundred and twenty of them at one whop."

Such attitudes of racial extremism have a long history in the Muslim movement. They are part of the psychological paraphernalia which nurture and sustain the movement and which provide the peculiar attractiveness for the social dissidents who fall under the hypnotic spell of Black Islam in the midst of a white Christian culture.

As is true of most social movements, the Black Muslims are not entirely dysfunctional. Some of their behavior contributes directly or indirectly to the improvement of the membership and thus to the community at large. For example, the rehabilitation of narcotic addicts and alcoholics is certainly socially functional, as is the teaching of thrift, obedience to the law, and employment skills and techniques. The organization's commitment to high standards of personal and group morality commend it to its most severe critics. Yet it is probably inevitable that a discourse addressed to the "extremist attitudes" of the movement cannot avoid some distortion. A more balanced account is offered in my book *The Black Muslims in America* (Boston: Beacon Press, 1961).

To the Black Muslims, every white man is a devil—the personification of evil. The white man is the genesis of evil and its sole beneficiary. In Muslim mythology, black man—"the Original Man," was created by Allah, the one true God. The

white man, however, is a "made thing," a beast, a synthetic
man called into being by Yakub, the evil principle which is
everywhere in opposition to peace, justice, and equality. Sometimes Yakub is personalized as the Prince of Devils, the eternal adversary to Allah.

Since the white man is the son of the devil, the white man
himself is a devil by nature and is incapable of doing good.
Ultimately the blue-eyed devils must be destroyed. Such is
the will of Allah.

Malcolm X's jubilation over the deaths of the white Geor-
gians is as honest as it is bizarre. The Black Muslims have never
pretended to love the white man or to wish him well. During
World War II the Muslims openly applauded American losses
in the Pacific because: (1) there would be fewer whites to
confront at the final Battle of Armageddon (to be fought
"here in the wilderness of North America"); and (2) Japanese victories were proof that a white civilization can be de-
feated by a non-white power.

In the early days of World War II a number of black nationalist cults came under the influence of the Japanese Black
Dragon Society—a fifth-column organization which sought to
exploit racial bitterness in the United States in the interest of
the Japanese. The society was founded by Major Satakata
Takahashi of the Japanese Imperial Intelligence in 1930 and
was estimated by the FBI to have a membership of 100,000 by
1942. Major units were in Chicago, St. Louis, Detroit, and
other cities in the Midwest.

One of the Negro cults most responsive to the Japanese
racial propaganda was the Black Muslims, then known as the
Temple of Islam. A Chicago newspaper reports that "Japanese
organizers frequently told the hundreds of followers of the
Allah Temple of Islam . . . of which Elijah Muhammad was
high priest: 'Be prepared for the day of reckoning with the

pale faces. When the day comes Japan will supply you all with guns.'"

The FBI conducted a series of raids on the Chicago South Side on September 22, 1942, and arrested twelve leaders and eighty members of three black nationalist cults including the Temple of Islam. The nationalists were charged with conspiring to promote the success of the enemy, making false statements to prospective draftees, and disrupting morale, causing mutiny.

A month later the twelve leaders (including Elijah Muhammad) were named in an eight-count indictment charging sedition and seditious conspiracy. The indictments centered around the black nationalists' alleged teaching that the Japanese and the "black men" in America were brothers: that Negroes should not permit themselves to be drafted to fight a war in which they had no stake; that if drafted against their wills, Negroes should ask for duty in the Pacific arena where they could defect to the Japanese; that if sent to Europe they should "shoot, everything white—in front and behind" to reduce the number of whites it would be necessary to kill later.[1]

J. Albert Woll, U.S. District Attorney who argued the case for the government, charged that the defendants "made statements as vicious as any ever uncovered by a grand jury."

Elijah Muhammad was sentenced to three years in the federal prison at Milan, Michigan. In prison, he promptly organized a Muslim temple among the Negro inmates, a practice since continued, and which has resulted in increasing perplexity for prison officials.

Perhaps the most bizarre extremism attributed to the Muslims came in Detroit in the 1930's, the formative years of the movement. This was the teaching that Allah required each

[1] Interview with Malcolm X.

Muslim brother to sacrifice four "Caucasian devils" as a condition of escape from the white man's oppression. It appears that the welfare workers in charge of the distribution of food during the depression years were especially hated. The accumulated resentments from having to stand in line for hours in order to receive handouts (frequently accompanied by insults) from the hated whites focused the Muslims' hostility upon the welfare workers as symbolic of the white man's total amorality. Had the devils not stolen the black men from their homes and families, enslaved them, humiliated them with a pseudo-citizenship, and then finally reduced them to begging for the very bread they worked without pay to produce?

The *Detroit Times* of November 22, 1932, reports the following incident:

> An Asiatic trend among the Negro dole recipients of the Elmwood district, noted at the time as a passing whim, today came back with horror to two women welfare workers on learning that the fanatical Robert Harris had intended them for human sacrifices as infidels. . . . Harris stated to the police that each of these was a "no good Christian," and that they would have been sacrificed if he knew [sic] where he could have found them.

Human sacrifice was not restricted to the Caucasian devils. Every Muslim was required to swear under oath that he would sacrifice *himself* or any of his family in obedience to the will of Allah as interpreted by the "Messenger" or leader of the cult. In this tradition Minister Malcolm X admonishes his Muslim brothers who are seeking respect and dignity:

> "Never be the aggressor;
> Never look for trouble.
> But if any man molests you,
> May Allah bless you!"

Indeed, the fiery Malcolm X insists that "if anyone comes to take advantage of you . . . *lay down your life!*" The theme of self-sacrifice and retributive violence is recurrent in the teaching of Elijah Muhammad. For example, he chides the Negro male for his passivity toward the white man's pursuit of Negro women. "If we are too cowardly to protect her against the human beasts," he declares, "we should kill ourselves and our women."

He is also impatient with the white man's notion of justice: "We must take things into our own hands," the Muslim Messenger insists. "We must return to the Mosaic law of an eye for an eye and a tooth for a tooth. What does it matter if ten million of us die? There will be seven million of us left."

The Black Muslim attitude toward the state, as presently constituted, is one of extreme negativity. In the first place, all black men are Asiatics, and Asia embraces all of the civilized world with the exception of Europe. Asia and Africa constitute a single continent. America is a part of "West Asia," as is illustrated by the fact that the native populations of North and South America were all nonwhite prior to the coming of the Europeans. Black men from Africa founded civilizations in America long before the coming of Leif Ericson or Christopher Columbus.

The Muslims deny that they are citizens of the United States. Rather they insist that as Muslims they are citizens of Asia. The white man in America is an intruder. He slaughtered the Indians, who are the rightful owners of the country, and set up a spurious democracy which included neither the Indians who were dispossessed of their land nor the "so-called Negroes" whose labor made America "the richest nation on earth."

Since the Muslims are not citizens they do not vote or otherwise participate in the responsibilities of citizenship. They refuse to bear arms for a country in which they are not

citizens "except at tax time and when the white man's enemies
have got his back to the wall." To be born in America is not
a guarantee of citizenship, Malcolm X declares: "A cat can
have kittens in an oven, but that doesn't make them biscuits . . .
You are either a citizen or you are not a citizen. No country
has citizenship by degrees."

A citizen is described as "one who can do what any other
citizen can do." Negroes are excluded by this definition for
"they are the only people in the world whose so-called 'citizenship' is qualified by geography, custom, tradition, the time
of day, and 'local sentiment!' "

In 1961, Wallace Delancey Muhammad, one of Elijah's six
sons and minister of his Philadelphia temple, was sentenced to
three years in prison for draft evasion. In permitting his son
to go to jail rather than to answer his draft call or accept alternative service in the Elgin State Hospital as a conscientious
objector, Muhammad sought to dramatize his insistence that
the Muslims not only will no longer fight the white man's bat-
tles, but they will not accept his alternatives. The American
Negro has been trained like a faithful dog, says Malcolm X.
"You tell him to bite the Germans, the Koreans. He will bite
anyone you say bite . . . Now when he comes back from biting
the Germans and the Japanese, you can hang his mother on a
tree and have his wife before his eyes and he will stand there
whimpering with his knees knocking and his tail between his
legs . . . that's what he's been trained to do."

The Muslims want a national state of their own. Muhammad states flatly that "there can be no peace in the world until
every man is in his own country." The white man's country,
he says, is in Europe. Nevertheless, the Muslims are willing to
divide the country with the white man, at least on a temporary
basis. In a recent address in Chicago the Muslim leader demanded that a separate territory be set aside for American
Negroes and that until this is done, Negroes should be ex-

empted from any form of taxation. "We must have separation or death," he has declared again and again.

The Muslims' leadership does not make clear how much territory is desired, or where it shall be. The area "west of the Mississippi and south of Denver" has frequently been mentioned. At least one Muslim minister has said that no less than twenty-five states will be enough.

The Black Muslims are bitterly anti-Christian, for Christianity is held to be the white man's most pernicious scheme for enslaving the nonwhite people of the world, while the white propagators of that religion relax in luxury and ease wherever they have found believing dupes. The Bible was originally a true and holy book, but "it has been tampered with" to serve the vicious interests of the white devils. Christianity itself is "a lie of the whole cloth, a 'spook' religion."

Muhammad describes this as "a perfect slave religion." It defers the so-called Negro's just aspirations for freedom, justice, and a share of the wealth he has helped to produce to some mythical heaven "over Jordan." Meanwhile, "the white man has made his heaven right here on earth." The Negro Christian minister is called the greatest enemy of his black brothers, for "he delivers his own people chained and bound to the tender mercies of the slavemaster—demanding that they love those who murder them wholesale."

The most prominent feature in the typical Muslim temple is a large pulpit mural featuring the Muslim interpretation of the relative merits of Christianity and Islam. On the right-hand side of the mural are depicted the Star and Crescent of Islam with the legend "Peace, Justice, Equality—Islam!" On the sinister side are shown the American flag, the Christian cross, and the swollen, mutilated body of a Negro hanging from a tree. Between these alleged symbols of Islam and Christianity, the question: "Which do you choose? Which will survive the War of Armageddon?"

The Muslims repudiate their "European slave names" (or surnames) and prefer to be known as "X"—James X, John 2X, Mary X, etc., the X in lieu of the family name which was lost when their fore-parents were enslaved and given "property titles" by the slavemaster. The X is also a symbol: it is a question mark, an unknown quantity directed to the attention of the white man. The time will come, says Muhammad, when "we will treat the white man the way he ought to be treated." As a farmer kills the worms and insects which spoil his crops, so must the black man be on the alert for the depredations of the Caucasian beast.

Bill Stout of Los Angeles CBS-TV quotes a Muslim leader as promising the whites "no torture—just annihilation. . . . We will not antagonize the white people. Some morning they will just wake up dead."

Traditional Negro leaders too have experienced a liberal measure of vituperation from the Muslims. Dr. Martin Luther King, referred to by the Muslims as "Martin Luther Queen," was ridiculed for "retreating from the portals of death in Alabama [for] the more lucrative haven of Atlanta," after setting the stage for a "bloody racial struggle soon to erupt in Alabama." Denounced as "the Darling of the South and Honey Boy of the North," King is challenged to "clear his conscience" by telling "the Negroes in America the truth—that they will never get . . . anything here on earth . . . until they are ready and willing to shed blood . . ." [2]

To the Muslims, Ralph Bunche is known as "the George Washington of Israel." They condemn him for arranging the Arab-Israeli armistice which "saved the Jews for annihilation."

Judge Thurgood Marshall is called the "Ugly American—the Negro man dedicated to serving his white masters." When he was with the NAACP, the Muslim press criticized Marshall

[2] *Los Angeles Herald-Dispatch*, January 9, 1960.

for being "the American Negro who has made a career of being an Uncle Tom," and who "has consciously or unconsciously accepted Zionism as a philosophy."[3] The NAACP and the nonviolent movements do not satisfy the Muslim concept of justice. They want the past to be rectified and the enslavement of their forefathers reimbursed in land and money. "We are not looking for crumbs," warns Malcolm X. "The black man in America is due not charity, but reparations," echoes the Muslim press. But Elijah Muhammad takes the final step.

"Today is the day of our separation from our slavemasters and *nothing* will stop it; for it is time," is Muhammad's warning to America. "Our hearts are glad and we weep with joy to know that it is *our time* to rule the world . . ."

In 1924, a faceless, ragged fanatic with a Charlie Chaplin moustache sat in a prison cell in Landsberg, Germany, and dictated a blueprint for the Third Reich. In *Mein Kampf*, Adolf Hitler told the world his ambitions for the restoration of the German empire and how it would be accomplished. The world ignored Adolf—to its sorrow. Adolf Hitler *did* accomplish the establishment of the Third Reich. Further, it required the combined armies of the Western World, and an incalculable quantity of human blood, to disestablish Hitler's monument to racistic nationalism and his own awareness of a personal manifest destiny.

It is not necessary to argue the possibility of a black nationalist *Putsch* in America, but it is fruitful to look at the facts. The world is in social revolution and the Negroes in America are part of that revolution. The student movement, Martin Luther King's movement, the new militancy in the churches (and paradoxically in art forms such as jazz), the mushrooming cults of black nationalism which keep springing up in the black ghettos of our great industrial cities, are

[3] *Los Angeles Herald-Dispatch,* January 30, 1960.

all shades of protest in a revolutionary spectrum. In New York City alone, at least twenty organizations operate under the aegis of black nationalism. Most of them are small. Some of them are noisy. But all of them accept as viable the possibility that black solidarity can and will reverse the existing political order.

Black nationalism is, in part, the Negro's counteroffensive against white nationalism. It is in part the fruit of oppression —the hate that hate produced. It is the glorification of Negro specificity, the transvaluation of the hated symbols of rejection. Blackness becomes a virtue. Whiteness becomes a symbol of weakness and depravity, political and social decadence.

This *mood ebony* stems in part from the Negro's felt need to identify with the newly emerging Afro-Asian states—people who are going somewhere, whose destiny it is to surpass and supplant the civilization of the white man. Negroes are resentful that here in democratic America, where they are alleged to be citizens by right of birth and contribution, they are begrudged and frequently denied the dignity and benefits of citizenship. They resent the cruel game of having to go into court or take to the sidewalks to prove again and again that their citizenship implies the most elemental human rights. They resent the white man's arrogant expectation that they should love him and be grateful for every belated, piddling concession to human dignity they can force from his iron fist. The feeling is widespread, though seldom articulated, that in spite of the fact that American Negroes more nearly approximate the white man's stated ideals, in greater numbers, than any other "subject people" on earth, this class of Americans may yet be the last people on earth to become truly free.

Elijah Muhammad has been shrewd enough to capitalize upon the anxiety and frustration of the masses. A man of intense hatreds and an uncanny ability to uncover the latent and carefully sublimated hostilities of the black masses, he is convinced of his personal messiahship. Further, Muhammad is a man of the most extraordinary charisma. It is probable that no one in the recent history of America has been able to attract such an all-encompassing loyalty from his followers as has this self-styled "Messenger of Allah." Cults like those of Father Divine and Daddy Grace are sometimes suggested as sociological parallels of the Muslim movement, but such suggestions are naïve and their inferences premature. The cultists are not required to lay down their lives for their leader or his teachings. Theirs is an escapist philosophy—a withdrawal from a world they find hostile and unrewarding to a make-believe world of peace and joy.

The Muslims plan to live in the world, reform the black race, survive the Armageddon, and establish a black theocracy. Elijah Muhammad's mission is to "cut and clear." He has come to tell the black man the truth about himself, his history, and Allah's plans for his future. He has come to expose the white man as a charlatan and a devil and to proclaim the "New Order."

> The root cause of today's confusion is that the time of the end of our enemies' [the devils'] power to rule and deceive our Nation has arrived. . . . NOW that ruling power is being interfered with by a Superior Power and Force, which will create a "New World," a New People, a New Order and a New Government.[4]

In the process of bringing about the new order, retribution must be demanded from the white man. Muhammad charges that "The white race . . . will never agree to divide America with us, though our blood is spilled on this soil. . . ." Hence the black man is enjoined to "put your brains to thinking for self; . . . your hands to working for self and your children; and fight like 'hell' with those who fight like 'hell' against

4 Interview with Muhammad.

you." He reminds his followers that "The white race is known to God and his prophets as Satan, the devil, the great enemy of Good, God, and his people . . . We now number seventeen million here in America . . . The wicked must be punished for their wickedness poured out upon us. . . ."

It is clear that the social policies of the Muslims are directed toward a racial contest between black men and white men. The overtones may be religious, for all is being done in the name of Allah—but the goals are patently social. Again and again Muhammad has stirred his followers to frenzy with the cry, "We must have some of this good earth! We must have land of our own!"

As the Muslim movement has consolidated its strength in the black ghettos, the Muslims have become increasingly restive. In the past year the Muslims have figured in incidents of violence in a dozen cities across the country: New York; Monroe, Louisiana; Atlanta; Saint Louis; Folsom, California; Washington, D.C.; Los Angeles, and other places. Recent incidents seem to become increasingly serious.

On March 5, 1935, two hundred Muslims rioted in a Chicago courtroom, and one policeman was killed and eleven others injured. Two Muslims were shot and forty were sent to prison. The struggle with constituted authority has continued in the streets, and especially in the prisons, ever since.

On April 27, 1962, a riot involving seventy-five policemen and several score Black Muslims left one Muslim shot to death and seven others injured by gunfire. Three policemen were hurt, one of whom was shot with his own gun. Since then the Black Muslims have been involved in a riot in the Lorton Reformatory outside of Washington, D.C.

The Muslims themselves are not always to blame, but their public image alone is often the precipitating spark which incites conflict. Their existence is a challenge to the existing order, and an indictment of its inadequacies.

The Muslim movement is a part of the sound and fury of social unrest. It has all the symptoms of neurotic social anxiety. It is a reaction to a perceived threat—a threat of political and social meaninglessness; but it is an extreme and bizarre reaction, a reaction which is disproportionate to any objective danger.

If we look carefully, we can see in the Black Muslim movement a microcosm of social behavior which has often characterized other segments of our culture. In the Muslim's intolerance, and in the preemptive place he has reserved for himself in the new order, we catch a vision of the existing order. In seeing the Muslims for what they want to be, we see ourselves for what we ourselves have sometimes been. In the words of Voltaire:

People will continue to commit atrocities as long as they believe in absurdities.

We can best understand and cope with the Black Muslim movement and its social implications when the larger society has abandoned the absurdities the Black Muslims have so recently adopted.

THE MEANING OF THE
NEGRO EXPERIENCE*

THE IMAGE OF A COMMODITY

One balmy afternoon in the late summer of 1619, a ship of the Royal Dutch Navy put about and tacked slowly into the harbor at Jamestown, Virginia. There was something strange about the appearance and the movement of the ship, something grotesque and foreboding. There was something repulsive and evil about the ship. The colonists waiting at the dockside experienced an unaccustomed shudder of apprehension as with an ominous rumble the long anchor chain uncoiled itself and brought the ship up fast against the wharf.

The captain of the Dutch ship caused the plank to be lowered and went ashore, followed by as motley a crew of sailors as had ever put to sea. Their provisions were gone; their water was gone. They had no money—but the captain explained that his ship carried a cargo well worth the provisions he wanted the settlers to exchange for it. It was a strange cargo. It was a cargo of men.

Lying in the darkness in the hold of the Dutch man-of-war were one hundred separate items of human flesh—chained ankle to ankle and wrist to wrist.

* Published in *Negro Digest*, March, 1963.

Braving the terrible stench and ignoring the cries of the suffering captives, by the dim light of a ship's lantern the Virginians picked out twenty and carried them ashore in chains. By that act they founded in democratic America a most peculiar institution; an institution about which Thomas Jefferson, himself a slaveholder, was to reveal the lacerations of his own conscience when he said, "I tremble for my country when I reflect that God is just; and his justice cannot sleep forever."

This was the first and most compelling image America has had of the Negro, the image of a commodity. A thing to be bought and sold or exchanged. A thing to be used in the production of wealth and power, comfort and ego-satisfaction for the benefit of those who own or have dominion over it.

With the clairvoyant wisdom which made him a great leader, George Washington had this to say about Negroes as a commodity: "I shall be happily mistaken if they are not found to be a very troublesome species of property ere many years have passed over our heads." George Washington has been gathered with the blest for 163 years, but that "troublesome species of property" first landed at Jamestown, Virginia, 343 years ago has perhaps proven Mr. Washington unhappily mistaken. For men are not "property," they are not commodities. They may not be bought and sold either on the slave block, or at the employment office, or in the courts, or at the bargaining table, or in the real estate office—for so long as they are, so long will they be "troublesome."

THE IMAGE OF AN EXPLORER

I have said that the early image most Americans have of the Negro in America is that of a commodity. Such was not the Negro's first role in this continent, nor within the present boundaries of this country. If no well-defined image consistent with his earlier experiences here has been developed, then

American history and racial understanding are poorer for the deficiency.

Had you been aboard the good ship *Pinta* on October 12, 1492, you would have noticed that among those rejoicing at the sighting of land was a small black man with the air of a scholar. He was Pedro Alonzo Nino, navigator of the flagship on which Columbus sailed. He was a Negro.

If you had marched with Balboa to the shores of the Pacific in 1519, you would have known Nuflo de Olano, one of the thirty Negroes included in his expedition. Or had you served with Navarez in 1527, you would have thrilled to the heroism of Estevánico, his Negro lieutenant who led an expedition into what is now Arizona and New Mexico, opening up the great Southwest for European conquest. Estevánico died fighting the Indians three hundred years before the first wagon train rolled westward from the Mississippi.

There were Negroes with the Spaniards in South America at the conquest of Peru; with the French in the settlement of the Mississippi Valley and the founding of Chicago. And in more recent times, even with Admiral Peary at the discovery of the North Pole.

But the image of the Negro as an explorer has not been sustained in the mind of America. Indeed, except for a handful of scholars, the Negro's role in discovery and exploration has remained "classified information."

THE IMAGE OF "UNCLE TOM"

Let us look quickly at two other historical images, both stereotypes from the slave period.

One is that of a gentle old man. His hair is white and woolly. His back is bent and his shoulders are rounded from a lifetime of genuflection. He observes a controlled deference to his betters and a supercilious indifference to the disapproval of his peers.

He is the medium through which communication passes from one class to another. He is the channel of distribution moving from the top to the bottom; he is the channel of information moving from the bottom to the top. His function is that of control and pacification—control of one class for the exploitation of another, and the pacification of one class for the protection of another.

His personal reward is the favor and the protection of the power structure, and they call him "Uncle—Tom." He is rewarded by his peers with suspicion, and hatred, and envy and fear. They rely upon his offices. (Indeed, they have no choice.) And they also call him "Uncle," but never to his face.

This is an image of the American Negro during the slave era. It is an image which has persisted into quite recent times. But it is an image which has been painfully eroded by the acids of social change.

The power structure has found the image of Uncle Tom to be a reliable agent of class control no longer. The Negro has found the image of Uncle Tom no longer capable of delivering even the old-time fractional benefits once surreptitiously lifted from the treasury of American citizenship. And further, the Negro today does not want anything that it takes an Uncle Tom to procure! *Today's Negro doesn't want charity. He does want a chance.* Uncle Tom is in bad health. He will soon be dead.

THE IMAGE OF A FREEDOM FIGHTER

On the second of October in 1750 there appeared in the *Boston Gazette* the following notice:

Ran away from his master WILLIAM BROWN . . . on the
30th of September last, a Negro Fellow, about 27 years of
Age, named CRISPUS, 6 feet 2 inches high, short curl's Hair,
his knees nearer together than common; had on a light
colour'd Bearskin Coat . . . blue yarn Stockings, and a checked
woolen shirt.

Whoever shall take up said Runaway, and convey him to
his . . . Master, shall have ten pounds . . . Reward . . .

History does not record whether the tall, knock-kneed Negro was ever "taken up" and returned to his master. But history has recorded the story of his martyrdom in the cause of
American freedom. It was the morning of March 5, 1770, that
the first American patriot died for a cause which remains so
dear to us all. A cause we have since defended successfully
many times, but a cause which is forever in jeopardy. For the
enemies of freedom are not always strangers from abroad. So
often they lie coiled within the bosom of democracy itself.

On a cold, blustery morning in March 192 years ago, a
company of British soldiers marched briskly up State Street
in the heart of downtown Boston. They had chosen State
Street because it was the principal street of what was then the
principal city in America. Their objective was to remind the
Americans of their continued subjection to the British Crown,
and to suppress with force any protestations of injustice or
any complaints about second-class citizenship. The Americans
had become very unhappy over being taxed while being denied representation in the government. Taxation without representation is galling to any self-respecting citizenry. Indeed,
no people could be reasonably expected to rejoice over a kind
of citizenship that required them to share responsibility while
privilege was withheld or deferred.

So it was that when the British soldiers swung arrogantly
up the street—resplendent in their scarlet jackets and arrogant

and confident in the superiority of their weapons—they could not have been surprised to find themselves challenged. To be sure, the challenge did not come from the class with vested interests, for that class was in league with the crown. The challenge came from the kind of men for whom principle is more important than wealth or station, or even personal security. The challenge came from men for whom the vision of equality and justice for all was a presently attainable objective.

Facing the British at the end of State Street was a handful of patriots. At the head was Crispus Attucks, a man who had established his personal freedom by running away as a youth, but who had now, as a man, returned to play his part in making a more complete freedom available for every American—including the master who had put a price on his head.

As the company of redcoats approached, Attucks turned to his supporters: "The way to get rid of these soldiers," he said, "is to attack the main guard."

With sticks and clubs and whatever weapons that came to hand, the Americans did attack. As Crispus Attucks led the charge, the British soldiers opened fire and he was first to fall. Three men died with Attucks at the Boston Massacre, but the struggle against tyranny had been joined, and ultimately the cause of freedom and justice did prevail. That America is today a free country testifies most eloquently to the availability of freedom when brave men work together in mutual confidence and determination. Today we are all free, but we are not yet *equally* free. We have been a long time completing the job begun in Boston so many years ago.

Crispus Attucks provides an image of the American Negro as a freedom fighter. Not many Americans remember Attucks. Fewer still not his race. His statue still stands on the Boston greensward along with those of other heroes of the American Revolution, for Attucks was the first American of any race to give his life in the cause of freedom. It is a pity that the editors of our children's textbooks do not know this or do not think it significant for these times.

There were many others to follow Attucks, for the freedom of America did not mean that all Americans were free. The struggle to be free was continued by Negro leaders like Nat Turner, Denmark Vesey, Gabriel Prosser, and others whose names are lost to history. Contrary to the widely circulated fiction of the Negro's docile acceptance of slavery, there were at least 109 *recorded* revolts in America between 1663 and 1864, a period of 201 years. In addition, there were no fewer than fifty-five revolts at sea during a similar period. Since it was the practice to suppress news about slave uprisings (lest they become infectious), it is reasonable to assume that scores of insurrections must have gone unrecorded.

The historical image of the Negro as a freedom fighter is certainly one which must be considered if the current struggle for freedom and dignity is to have perspective. We need to talk about the past because the present has no meaning except with reference to the past and to the future. America cannot hope to understand the complex image of the contemporary Negro unless there is a historical screen against which to project it. We cannot understand the sit-ins, the freedom riders, the Black Muslims, the NAACP, or even the Urban League except in the context of antecedent behavior.

The keys to the Negro's resentments, his forbearance, his hostility, his love, his patience, his weariness with waiting, his resignation, and his determination are all there in his "previous condition," but the full story of his previous condition is not a mere tale of abject servitude.

There has not been enough said about the past. The Negro's strengths and his weaknesses are reflected in the images he has of himself and others have of him. Most Negroes have displayed a childish squeamishness about probing Negro history. They have been too afraid that research might lead to some dark jungle and that the Negro would be "further disgraced." They have been too afraid of being deprived of certain convenient excuses for comfortable mediocrity they seem to enjoy in a segregated society.

The white man has preferred not to disturb the Negro's past because he wants no new challenge to his moral consciousness, no new feelings of guilt. He does not wish to risk the possibility that some out-of-date conclusions may on reexamination require some adjustment in his habits of thinking or patterns of behavior. It sometimes appears that Negros and whites are joined in a conspiracy of silence for their mutual protection against social and moral embarrassment.

THE THREEFOLD MYTH

The racial chauvinists in the South are far from silent. In centennial celebrations all over the old Confederacy, the diehards are resurrecting the pale gray ghost of the Civil War. They are doing so with the meek compliance of the North (and very often with the financial and technical assistance of agencies of the federal government which might well be occupied with more plausible and more socially profitable undertakings). The Civil War image of the South being offered today to American's innocent and unsuspecting children (and to their unprotesting parents) is very often fraudulent, fictional, irrelevant, and inane. It is an image which carefully ignores the fundamental issues over which the Civil War was fought. White supremacy is busily engaged in beating a dead horse to make him win a race that is over. The resurrection of the "grand illusion" would be pathetic, if ours were a more sophisticated (or even a more moral) society. Unfortunately the trinal myth of the Negro's "inherent inferiority," his "satisfaction with things-as-they-are," and the white man's "good intentions" to be executed by his own initiative bye-and-bye, is still supported by a formidable cult. If the Negro continues his attacks upon the segregated institutions of the North, the Cult of the Grand Illusion is certain to grow larger, at least for a time. Bigotry must have an image of its victim consistent with its aim.

THE NEGRO'S SELF-IMAGE

The Negro has some images of himself. Whereas outsiders tend to see "one" Negro—a composite, stereotyped image of "the race"—Negroes see themselves as a multifaceted American subgroup with many "images," some good, some indifferent, some bad. What is the Negro's image of "the Negro in America"? It depends upon which Negro you ask:

It is the dramatic image of Thurgood Marshall pleading the cause of human justice before the high court of the nation and the conscience of the people.

It is the image of a shoeshine boy in Nashville refusing to scramble for a 10¢ tip flipped into the gutter at his feet.

It is the image of Martin Luther King challenging a hate-filled and often violent post-Christian society to relearn the great principles of the Sermon on the Mount—showing them how to win over hatred with love and how to overcome violence with humble faith and self-restraint.

It is the image of Elijah Muhammad—black messenger of a black God, calling the disconsolate and arming them with hatred. A bitter man this Muhammad, and one tired of waiting for his share of America, leader of the militant Black Muslims who return hatred for hatred, insult for insult, blow for blow. A black supremacist in search of victory over white supremacy.

It is the image of Jackie Robinson "maintaining speed while shifting gears"—moving on from a brilliant career in sports to an executive position in a major American business enterprise.

It is the image of Ralph Bunche doing a job for his country and losing his racial identity in the process.

It is the image of Ralph Boston and Wilma Rudolph saving the day for America on the Olympic fields of the world.

It is the image of Malcolm X, strident apostle of black nationalism, preaching in the black ghettos, debating at the universities, haranguing on the street corners, shouting from the television screen and the eleven o'clock radio shows—"Think black! Buy black! Stay black! And beware the white man's phony integration!"

It is the image of Louis Armstrong, the ambassador with a horn at his lips; and of Chubby Checker, teaching the world a new twist.

It is the image of nine little teenagers at Little Rock's Central High School ignoring the insults, accepting the hot soup poured on their heads, the lighted cigarettes dropped down their backs, the screaming mothers, the bombs and the dynamite while the world recoiled in horror—and then cheered and cheered and cheered.

It is the image of college youth all over America—sitting in, riding in, wading in, reading in, kneeling in—and sometimes having to crawl out—going to jail accepting their punishment, and then sitting in again.

It is the image of the Urban League executives working quietly but persuasively with the concerned and responsible citizens of the great metropolises—trying to make urban living better for all the people irrespective of race or creed.

The Negro's image of the Negro is sometimes one of a steadily increasing middle class, with all of the status pretentions of the white middle class. It is the image of a burgeoning "black bourgeoisie" striving mightily to become totally assimilated into the mainstream of America and suffering massive frustration for having failed.

There is another image—one of hundreds of thousands of

slum dwellers caught in the deteriorated inner circle of the great cities of America—the black ghettos, ringed with bands of steel—political steel, economic steel; the cold, hard steel of prejudice.

It is an image of crime: drug addiction, alcoholism, burglary, desertion, assault, prostitution, gambling, and murder.

It is the image of unemployment, destitution, bitterness, hopelessness, disease, and resignation.

It is the image of extreme poverty in the midst of an affluent society.

It is the image of a raw deal.

It is the image of a keg of powder with a six-inch fuse.

THE IMAGE OF A HUNGRY MAN

The most compelling image I know of the contemporary Negro is that of a "hungry man."

This is the era of the "hungry man" to some, "The Abominable Hungry Man." The hungry man is the symbol of very many millions of people who are hungry for food, hungry for understanding, hungry for freedom and self-determination. But most of all—hungry for the dignity without which a man is a thing, a chattel and a commodity. The dignity without which a man is a misfit, a monstrous joke in his own eyes. A broken vessel in the eyes of God.

The sign of the hungry man is his determination, his dedication, his quiet insistence, and his courage. It is the sign of the search for dignity.

The Negro is like a certain hungry man who, though an uninvited guest, has seated himself as unobtrusively as possible at the banquet table of America. Since he was not invited, he has come of his own accord. Since no place was set for him, he has brought his own utensils. This makes him abominable, for no diner of good breeding comes unasked and then brings to the table his own knife and fork.

But this hungry man has come to eat. He feels his right to be there, for he has shared in the cultivation of the fields, in the production of the food, and in the protection of the common heritage that is America from the hostile incursions of our common enemies who would have put us *all* to the sword.

The hungry man is seated at the banquet table of America. He sees the rich viands passed back and forth in front of him as the opulent diners "officially" ignore his presence and make merry—eating and drinking to satiety. I say that the hungry man is officially ignored, for behind the convivial façade, the light and pleasant chatter, the clever exchange of anecdotes, there is an uneasy awareness that the hungry man is about to become a problem. He refuses to go away. He is dressed in evening clothes like all the other diners, and he sits there like a man who is determined to be served. He is quiet and dignified, but he has big shoulders. He has big hands.

The problem: *How to pacify him with the least cost and inconvenience. How to get him out—or get him served without a commotion that may well spoil the banquet for everybody.*

But the hungry man isn't leaving. He has come to eat. He has come to stay. He has taken his seat at the banquet table he worked so faithfully to help prepare. *He is sitting-in until he's served.*

This is his moment in the struggle for freedom and dignity throughout the world, a world in which men have been enslaved by men for so long that the orderly processes of history have been disturbed and the moral nature of man has been grotesquely distorted. The Negro's prevailing self-image is in general reflected in the determination that if the most desirable values of our society have been consistently preempted on the arbitrary basis of race, then the forces which sustain that arrangement ought to be challenged. His struggle is nothing more than what America ought to expect of its citizens. The self-respecting contemporary Negro is determined that color shall no longer be the criterion by which his opportunities and his personal dignity and worth are to be measured—neither in the South, nor in the North, nor anywhere else in this democratic society.

Shackles may be made of iron: lacerating the flesh and restraining the body. But there are shackles of custom and tradition: the prejudice which binds the mind, kills the spirit, and deforms the soul of anyone it touches. Negroes will no longer submit to bigotry. America can no longer expect it of them.

THE ESSENCE OF THE NEGRO

Almost a hundred years have passed since the Fourteenth Amendment recognized the image of the Negro to be the image of a citizen. A hundred years is a very long time for a people in an equalitarian democracy to fail to make fully effective the normal expectations of citizenship. Our national behavior has not been consistent with the very reasonable expectation that the highest values be available on equal terms to all. Instead of working to eliminate causes we have been expending our resources on symptoms. Instead of policing the forests we have been dissipating our energies running from brush fire to brush fire—too late and with too little water. Instead of looking for essence we have been looking at images and trying to construct programs on sands that shift with each passing wind.

An image is a chimera. It is always changing—always appearing differently from different perspectives. An image is always reflecting the vicissitudes of the times, the pressures and opportunities of the moment. It is always partly the creation of the man who perceives it.

Image is what you see. Essence is what you feel. In trying to deal with an image, one may miss the broader opportunity of encountering a person.

I have to say that there is no one "image" of the Negro upon which sincere people should attempt to base their social attitudes. One can no more generalize about twenty million black Americans than one can about twenty million white Americans.

Image is what you see. Essence is what you feel. Human images differ from day to day, from group to group, and within the group—every group. *Human essence is the same in all men—all the time.* It is that peculiar quality which makes a man a man and separates him from all other possibilities. It is essence with which we ought to be concerned, for if we were, there could be but one image, and that would be the image of America!

BLACK NATIONALISM AND
CHRISTIAN CONSCIENCE*

In Muhammad's Temple of Islam No. 2, far down in the Chicago South Side in the heart of the great black ghetto, there is a mural on the wall behind the lectern. It is not a representation of Jesus in the role of the Good Shepherd comforting the distressed of his flock in the warmth of His bosom; nor of the wise men making their way to the stable of Bethlehem; nor yet of the magnificent sunrise shattering the darkness of the cavern of death at Easter.

In Muhammad's Temple of Islam in the Chicago ghetto, and in seventy-odd temples in seventy-odd black ghettos scattered about America, the murals behind the lecterns tell another story. And they ask a vital question: "Which do you choose: Peace, Justice and Equality in black Islam, or the continued terror and humiliation of a second-class existence under Christianity—the *white man's* religion?"

Which do you choose?

If you have ever been into one of Muhammad's mosques, the crucial question stays with you and burns itself into your consciousness. Despite the Muslims' idealization of Islam and the crude and premature judgment of Christianity, despite the black man's devotion and fidelity to a familiar way of life, the

* Published in *Concern*, Sept. 15, 1963.

question intrigues him. "If the options were valid," he asks himself, "which would I really choose?"

Perhaps 100,000 American Negroes, practically all of them ex-Christians, Protestants, Catholics, and others, have chosen Islam—black Islam as it is interpreted by Elijah Muhammad, the self-styled Messenger to the "Black Nation," lost and enslaved in "the wilderness of North America." Additional thousands have abandoned traditional styles of life to affiliate with other black nationalist groups: the Drums, the Hearts of Africa, the Yoruba Temple, the First Africa Corps; the Moorish Americans, Jamiyat III Fallah, the United Sons and Daughters of Africa, the United African Nationalist Movement, and many lesser-known cults of black nationalism.

There is little evidence that the Christian church has been heretofore concerned about the black nationalist—either as a movement of the socially distressed searching for an escape from the suffocating bigotry of the society at large, or as men and women who once were counted within the Christian tradition. It is high time the church took note.

I

The Negro has become an urban dweller. He has bartered one set of uncertainties for another. He has abandoned the plantation cabin only to end up in the black ghetto of the most indescribable slums. He has fled the unemployment of the South only to end up in the bread lines of the North. The Ku Klux Klan has its counterparts in the "gentlemen's agreements" between labor and management, among real estate dealers, politicians, and others within the power structure that deny the Negro jobs, housing, and access to public accommodations.

Everywhere school segregation and police brutality and hostility toward Negroes are the same. What is not the same is the Negro's attitude about his lot. The old paladins to which he looked for rescue—the church and the "good people"—have been somewhat less than swift in taking up his cause. They have been preoccupied with other causes from the pleasant suburbs to which they have fled to escape the ugly reminders of the American dilemma.

It came inevitably to the Negro that if he were going to be saved he would have to save himself. Suddenly it was evident that in the mid-twentieth century, on the threshold of the Age of Space and the precipice of eternity, neither the church, nor the law, nor the white man had yet effected his release from social bondage and did not seem impressed with an urgency to do so.

The whole world was in radical metamorphosis. Undemocratic institutions all over the world were being abandoned. Only in South Africa, Portuguese Angola, and the United States did the white man maintain a studied obliviousness to the black man's plea for freedom.

Massive anxiety has been the characteristic mood of America's Negro population since the closing stages of World War II. American Negroes have witnessed the lengthening processions of nonwhite peoples advancing to the bar of justice and being handed their certificates of freedom. They have asked themselves again and again, "When will our time come? When will we be free? When will our American citizenship become de facto as well as de jure?"

For all these questions the Black Muslims had an answer, "Never!" The white man, the Muslims say, is a devil by nature. He is incapable of loving any who are not white. His religion is a religion of bondage—a fiendish strategy that successfully enslaved all of the nonwhite peoples of the world and pacified them with the spurious promise of freedom and equality in some fictitious heaven after death.

The Black Muslims are an example of the catastrophic anxiety that can overwhelm a people when they are bereft of hope and their lives are devoid of meaning. Unlike the more stable elements in the Negro subgroup, the Muslims' reaction to the feeling of dereliction and abandonment has been sufficiently violent to suggest a complete disassociation from the larger society as the only means of coping with the white man's intransigence.

In the Muslim community the lamp of resentment with its flame of black hatred is carefully tended against the Day of Armageddon. Theirs is the hate that hate produced, or so they believe, for if the white man does not hate the black man, then why has he degraded him for so long? The discovery of the "truth about the white man," i.e., his demonic state, his hatred of the Negro, and his perversion of Christianity to support a racist philosophy, is the central fact that makes the Black Muslim movement a viable expression of America's bitterest and most disillusioned Negroes.

To cope with the facts as they see them, the Black Muslims have sought to restore to human relationships the archaic philosophy of "an eye for an eye, a tooth for a tooth." Malcolm X demands of his followers: "Never be the aggressor. Never look for trouble; but if any man molests you, may Allah bless you!"

Ten years after World War II, Muhammad and his Black Muslims became news. They became news because the ferment in the ghetto began to produce a rumbling—an ominous rumbling that threatened the racial façade which has so long obscured democracy. The Black Muslims did not produce the rumblings, but they became the symbols of racial unrest that could explode into a kind of civil violence that would make the infamous Red Summer of 1919 pale by comparison. We are fortunate that, for the most part, instead of civil violence we have had civil disobedience, and that although there has been blood, the determined march for civil rights has not yet become bloody.

The Black Muslims are a part of the Negro's all-out struggle for freedom. They represent the extreme right wing of the Negro's spectrum of protest. They do not want integration; they want complete separation. They want no part of anything associated with the white man. They want a complete separate economy in a separate territory under the hegemony of black men. They want separation because they question the white man's ability to adjust to an integrated society, or even a pluralistic one. They do not accept nonviolence as an effective principle of negotiation.

II

It is gratifying that the Christian conscience has not abandoned the thousands of Negroes who follow Elijah Muhammad, and the thousands of others, who in their despair and helplessness, are ready to turn to black nationalism and in consequence to a certain and predictable fate. The church ought to be concerned about black nationalism in general and the Black Muslims in particular, not only because the Muslims espouse a schedule of values in conflict with that which we believe to be highest and best for the good life, but also because through misfeasance, and malfeasance and nonfeasance, we have contributed heavily to the creation of attitudes of black nationalism. Permit me to cite the following examples:

1. The Black Muslims are guilty of a gross distortion of history. They teach their children that all the significant contributions to human civilization were made by black men. "Black Man" is alleged to have been the "Original Man," first to populate the planet Earth, first to know and call upon the One True and Living God (whose right and proper name is "Allah"), first to cultivate the earth and found civilizations.

Surprising though the realization will be to some, we are no less extreme in our advocacy of racial primacy in human history. Despite the paucity of scientific information about the origins of the human species and the details of ancient civilizations, our children were taught that the worthwhile contributions to civilization have been made by white men and that the inevitable supremacy of the white race over all others is an indubitable fact of history.

2. The Black Muslims preach, and presumably they are prepared to practice, a gross and blatant racism. They hold black man alone to be capable of moral behavior and worthy of divine love and affection.

In an inversion of the traditional color symbols for good and evil, the Muslims have identified the white man with whatever is wrong, dirty, or immoral. Black they say is divine, hence all black men participate in divinity. Allah himself is a "Supreme Black Man," first among equals in a black theocracy.

In the world view of the Black Muslims, theirs is a manifest destiny, and in their anticipated fulfillment of history there is no place for the white man. When the Muslims are in power, says Elijah Muhammad, "We will treat the white man the way he ought to be treated." Presumably the Muslims have learned by experience and observation.

The Muslim leaders define their task as bringing to consciousness the significance of being black in a world where the white man is vastly outnumbered and where the disproportion is very rapidly increasing. The final historical denouement is the promised battle of Armageddon to be fought, not in some mystical valley of Asia Minor, but "right here in the wilderness of North America." It is to be the concluding battle of history—the final confrontation between the black and white peoples of the world.

In the eyes of the Muslim, racial integration is not a viable

issue. The Muslim views integration as a trick, another strata-
gem of the white man to insure his own self-preservation.
Elijah Muhammad dismisses the issue of physical proximity to
demand impatiently, "Why integrate with a dying man? The
white man's doom is sure." The nonwhite people of the world
need only wait around to pick up the pieces of history and go
on from there, Muhammad declares.

Christians may well view with alarm so vicious and cate-
gorical a racist philosophy. But then the thoughts are not
entirely new, for there are parallels in the larger society. A
full-blown white supremacy, quite as vicious and fanatical as
the incipient black supremacy fermenting in the ghettos, has
ordered our religious, social, political, and personal lives as
long as we can remember. Contemporary Negroes have been
conveniently identified as divinely decreed hewers of wood
and drawers of water, cursed of God and man. Relegated to
the outer darkness of this society, they are confined to the
ghetto, locked out of the churches, and generally made to
feel that they are excluded from whatever destiny—manifest
or otherwise—for which the white man believes himself to
have been chosen.

3. A serious aspect of Black Islam is that practically all of
its recruits are drawn from the Christian churches or from
families with a Christian heritage. No single group of people
anywhere received the Christian message with more fervor or
greater faith than did the Negroes of America. In black America the Christian heritage is deep and meaningful, and even to
this day the superficialities of the religion of modernity have
made no serious inroads into the Negro churches. God and
the church have been the Negro's comfort against the psychological devastation incident to being black under a white
hegemony.

And yet we are witnessing the peculiar paradox of Christians abandoning their faith to become Black Muslims. Chris-

tian pastors have become Muslim ministers. Devout laymen have succumbed to a strange doctrine of bitter hatred and black supremacy.

A hundred thousand followers of Elijah Muhammad means that 100,000 Christians or potential Christians have despaired of finding meaning for their lives in the churches of America. In some cities the Muslims have picketed the Christian churches, passing out anti-Christian literature urging the black Christians to abandon the white man's religion and return to Islam, "the natural religion of the black man."

The churches have not responded except to demand the Muslims' arrest or to complain that such a "Communist" organization ought to be investigated. To my knowledge there have been no positive programs aimed at meeting the Muslim movement, and more importantly the implications of the movement, on its own ground. Indeed, most Christians know little if anything about the Black Muslims, and care less. We are too busy with being busy to have time for the little holes in the dikes that separate our backyards from the sea.

4. Muslim discipline is strict; and Muslim morality is exemplary. Delinquency among Muslim children is almost unheard of. There is no smoking, no drinking, no carousing in black Islam, and this is the more remarkable because 95 per cent of the Muslim following is recruited from the black ghetto, where whiskey is the poor man's psychiatrist and carousing is his escape from the terror of reality.

The Muslim woman graces and dignifies the home, and the Muslim male orders and protects it. The Muslims have adopted the Christian concept of morality and made it work. "We can not build a great nation with an undisciplined people," declares Muhammad. Neither can the church.

5. It used to be a Christian tradition to go into the hedges and byways in search of souls for Christ. Once it was not uncommon for Christian denominations even to compete with

each other. All this is passé. The man in need of salvation today must make it to the church on his own—and even then
he may not get in.

But the Muslims have taken over the rich reserve abandoned by the churches. In the pool halls, the barbershops, the
chicken shacks, the jails and the prisons they have reaped an
impressive harvest—not for Christ, but for Muhammad. "We
are not concerned with what a man was yesterday," says Malcolm X. "We are interested in what he can be tomorrow."

The Muslims are organized in every major prison in the
United States. In their local temples they welcome the dope
addicts, the prostitutes, the petty thieves, and the ex-convicts.
They clean up these social outcasts, give them jobs, and make
Black Muslims out of them. On the day of Armageddon no
one will care much who was who.

III

The Christian church ought to care about the day of Armageddon. As sophisticated Christians, we know the Muslim
Armageddon to be a fantasy among the myriads of fantasies
which compose the mythological fabric of the Muslim world
view. That is not the point. What is important is that Armageddon and indeed the whole ideological panoply of black
nationalism in America is an implied indictment of the white
nationalism around which our society is structured. The
church is a part of the social structure and must share the judgment brought against it. But the church is no more (and no
less) guilty than any other social institution.

The Black Muslims say that Christianity is a "white man's
religion." We know that it is not. But we have behaved as
though it were. We have done so not out of malice, not out
of any teachings inherent in the doctrines of the church, nor

out of any innate incapacity to be inclusive in our love for mankind. Our failure is a failure of vigilance. We have been narcotized by the spectacles and the wondrous inanities of our culture, and we have awakened belatedly and found the idols of the tribe ensconced in our churches and in our personal lives. We have capitulated to the secularizing influences of our culture. The Black Muslims are the bitter fruit that grows on the vine we planted.

BREAKERS AHEAD!*

Let America make haste! It is considerably later than we think . . . The condition of the American Negro is today's bitterest joke about freedom and justice.

As the wheel turns, life becomes progressively more complex, and meaningful survival, national and personal, seems more and more like one long gauntlet between Scylla and Charybdis. At least this is true for many people. Tension and anxiety are so much a part of our daily lives that we accept them as normal conditions of existence. (Yet their toll in the disintegration of personality and related problems must be very high indeed!) Recently I heard a woman express her gratification at being able to get through 1963. "It was an awful year," she said. "So many problems. *So many tragedies.*"

Nineteen sixty-three was indeed a fateful year for Americans and for most of the people of the world. For us, it was a year burdened with the kind of events which illustrate the corporate personality of a whole people, divulge their national character, and reveal their strengths and weaknesses. There is no need to catalogue the burden of events with which the year just past was invested, for they were of a sort that in-

* Published in *Negro Digest*, May, 1964.

volved almost every American, personally or at least vicariously. Take the mine disaster in Pennsylvania, for example—a tragedy which reminded us so poignantly that a man's life is not his alone. It belongs at least in part to his family and his friends, and even to the larger society. Even among the most lowly and the most deprived, life is a value with which men are loathe to part. No matter how poor they are, no matter what they do for a living, no matter how utterly wretched their existence, men want to live for themselves and for those they love and cherish. Men want to live because tomorrow the reversal may come. Tomorrow the weight of the centuries may be lifted from their shoulders and some new Atlas may be chosen by the Fates to bear the burdens of the world for a time. And society, of course, has a stake in the preservation of individual lives, although we sometimes behave as if the contrary were true.

There was the tragedy of unemployment in Harlem and West Virginia; the Vietnam incident in far-off Indochina; the murder of the innocents in Birmingham. All America watched the pageant of the Great March of Protest on the capital city of the United States. There was the Dallas incident—a brutal tale in which a man marked for greatness and an uncontested place in history was shot down like a common thief in the most fantastic tragicomedy of modern times, while a brave, heroic woman showed the world that the dignity of courage need not be subsumed by grief.

Looking back, Janus-like, we must concede that 1963 was a year of hatred and violence, of murder, and fear and invective. But interstitially, it was also a year of heroism, and courage and hope. Few were sorry to see the old year close. All of us are apprehensive about the portents of 1964.

One aspect of the heritage of the American people has been an individualism which has produced on the one hand a rugged independence and a hallowed determination to avoid interference with whatever is not of primary personal concern to the individual. Because we have (until fairly recent times) enjoyed a certain isolation from the rest of the world that has functioned to insulate us from most of the world's problems, the occasion for *personal* involvement in the personal struggles of people elsewhere in the world has not been forcefully presented. Because America is itself a giant country with plenty of space and elbowroom for all, we have not been required to take notice of our neighbors. This same philosophy of laissez faire has operated at home to produce for most of us an obliviousness of the problems and accomplishments of any outside the primary groups to which we belong. As a consequence, we have maintained our own privacy (and permitted a like privacy to others) at the expense of an appalling ignorance of the very factors which threaten the values we cherish so much. While the most influential Americans have commuted to the suburbs with averted eyes, poverty and disease, hatred and hostility have filled the vacuums they never permitted themselves to see. Furthermore, because we have so frequently abdicated responsibility to irresponsible people, we have as frequently reaped a harvest of incredibly bad government, the primary intent of which is to maintain the status quo, i.e., the ignorance and impotence of the responsible in order that the self-aggrandizement of the irresponsible may proceed unhampered. The irony of it all is that the most inept rulers always rule in the name of "the people," while "the people" themselves are modestly silent and far above it all.

It is time for the responsible men of this country to make an intelligent appraisal of what is happening in America, for if we do not, it is inevitable that our most important values will be lost by default. Ours is a society experiencing the most rapid rate of change in its fundamental values of any society anywhere at any time in history. Some of this change is good; some of it needs to be evaluated. Some of it is disfunctional to our national purpose and to our survival as a free and independent society. Our principal danger lies in the fact that in the turbulence of the social flux some changes are imperceptible and go undetected until they are accomplished facts.

Another danger is that in learning to live with modern technology we have become so acclimated to change as to accept it at face value in most areas of our lives. We have accepted the dictum that "you can't turn back the clock" as if all change were progress, and as if we have nothing to say about what changes we shall have and what changes we shall avoid. We behave as if the world were a huge mechanism, already wound and rolling when we got on, and we are powerless to deflect it from its course of aimlessness and guide it in the direction of more creative realities. It is probably true that none of us can stop the world and get off, but each of us can play a decisive part in determining where it is going.

Nineteen sixty-four is going to be a crucial year in the fate of the world and the people of the United States. If we are to be participants in the drama of our lives rather than mere objects to be manipulated and shoved here and there by the patterns of events, then we must concern ourselves seriously about some of the issues which are before us as individuals, citizens, and sustainers of the national purpose which embodies the American self-image. I do not intend to attempt an exhaustive analysis of what is wrong with America, nor is such a critique indicated. But perhaps it may still be profitable to talk about some of the problems with which we are certain to be confronted. They are not problems which we can solve as individuals, but in thinking about them and talking about them we help to create a climate more nearly conducive to a realistic expression of the will of the people.

The category of possibilities is broad, but I have selected four areas which I believe will illustrate the gravity of condi-

tions now playing an important part in the shaping of our lives
and the circumstances under which we live.

1. TECHNOLOGY

Philosophers have argued that the only persistent thing in
life, the only thing that does not change, is change itself. The
world is forever in the process of change. People change. Institutions change. Patterns of behavior change. So there is
nothing very new in the idea of change or the experience of
it. What *is* new to contemporary Americans and to most of
the rest of the world is the *rate* of change—the speed with
which familiar institutions, accepted ideas, and hardened patterns of behavior are passing out of existence to be replaced
by new and unfamiliar entities. History becomes increasingly
irrelevant as a guide for solving the problems we must face
today and tomorrow. For example, what can we learn from
Napoleon, or Clausewitz, or Pershing, or even Eisenhower
and MacArthur about the war we seem to feel we have to
fight tomorrow or the day after? History used to teach that
war was a political instrument, that wars could be fought and
won, peace restored, and existing international arrangements
altered to the profit and glory of the victor. How archaic is
this lesson in 1964!

What can we learn from the political presuppositions of the
nineteenth century, or even of the thirties and forties of the
present century? We can learn something, to be sure, from
the fundamentals, but the specifics of twenty years ago have
receded into the realm of the irrelevant. Today the destiny of
America is irrevocably linked to the destiny of every nation
in the world. Because the people of India and a thousand other
unnamed communities of Asia and Africa and South America
are dying of hunger, we are uneasy with our swollen granaries
and rotting potatoes. Because the people in the Congo, or in

Vietnam, or in the Negev Desert, or on the island of Cyprus want to fight each other, our far-flung armies and probing naval units are restless. Colonialism and racial oppression in South Africa and Angola make us anxious and concerned. We are not an island unto ourselves. For better or for worse, for as long as we can tell and as far as we can see into the future, we are indissolubly linked to the mainland of human history —to all nations, all races, all religions. Their accomplishments are our own; their problems of survival are our problems of survival—clearly even now, and even more decisively in the future.

This is the era of the machine. This is the era in which we find ourselves confronted with two infinities—the infinity of space and the infinity of nuclear war. The chief instrument by which we propose to probe both of these infinities is the machine. Hence, technology has come to bear upon our lives in so many ways and with such force as to give it preeminence among the problems with which responsible Americans will have to deal in 1964 and the succeeding years, if any. Ninety per cent of all the scientists who ever lived are living today, and they are creating for us a world which threatens to exceed our present, political, moral, and economic capacities. I do not believe with the determinists that technology is a force with a life of its own directing the destinies of its creators. Men do not have to go where technology directs them; they do not have to do whatever technology suggests that it is possible to do. The imperatives of technology *can* be resisted. But *are* they?

It is common knowledge that technology has long since taken over the arms race. We build bigger and better bombs for no other reason than that it is technologically possible to do so. For years we have had a decisive overkill capacity. Today we have 126 times the nuclear might needed to annihilate completely any potential aggressor in any quarter of the world. It is not for political advantage or national security that we continue to install bigger and more fearsome weapons systems. It is because an escalating technology tells us it is possible to do. But technology says nothing about the moral implications of our weapons systems or what we plan to do with them. We are in danger of becoming prisoners of the very machines we have created to insure our freedom and survival—or at least to be certain that no one else is free or survives.

In *Fail-Safe*, that disturbing novel dealing with our automated defense system and the possibility of accidental war, the authors describe our helplessness to prevent an unprovoked nuclear attack against a potential enemy once a signal has been fed into the machinery by the most unlikely accident—or by technological miscalculation. In his book *Kill and Overkill*, Ralph Lapp tells about a recent accident in which an American bomber dropped a thermonuclear device on North Carolina. The device had six "foolproof" safety locks on it to prevent accidental detonation. According to the Strategic Air Command, none of these six safety locks could possibly be triggered by accident. When the device was examined after being hurled to the earth, five of the "foolproof" safety switches had been triggered.

But the problem of thermonuclear technology does not confine itself to accidental war. It is a problem that searches out our fundamental values. Technology is a tool, an instrument. Under proper control and direction, its function is to serve man, not to dominate him. It is a means, the search for the one best way in the pursuit of efficiency. We are in danger of making technology an end in itself—the prime value of American life.

Along with the blessings of increased efficiency, technology has also given us scandalous surpluses of foods, mountainous scrap heaps of obsolete machinery, and an ever-increasing population of unemployed and unemployable men and women. We shall have to concern ourselves with the problems of technology, and quickly, while there is yet time. We need human engineering to cope with the increasing problems created by our technologists. At a time when we are in need of all the brains we can get, we may find it expedient to welcome back the so-called "eggheads" we have so perfunctorily dismissed from time to time.

2. ECONOMICS

A second problem is that of our economic order. It is in part related to the problem of technology, as I have indicated. We now have the capacity to produce all the goods and services needed by Americans, but not all Americans have what they need of what we can produce. One fifth of all Americans live at or below the level of poverty. There are areas in this country which are quite as "undeveloped" as any in Asia or Africa. The need and the poverty, the abject misery saddling the slums of affluent America, tell a familiar tale of the inequities of the distribution of wealth in this democratic society. Fifty million Americans do not have enough to eat. They are, in addition, undereducated, underemployed, and confined to the ghetto. If we do not move to rectify these conditions, we must inevitably reap the consequences in crime and delinquency, the lowering of health standards, wasted manpower, hostility and social revolution. Einstein previewed our economic predicament shortly before his death when he declared that the individual has become more conscious than ever of his dependence on society. But he views this dependence not as a positive asset or as a protective force, but rather as a threat to his natural rights and to his economic existence.

We shall have to come to terms with the probability that millions of today's unemployed will never again enjoy sustained employment. It is not a question of whether or not they *want* to work. These are human rejects, the victims of the technological revolution now in progress. We are more fortunate than some countries. W. H. Ferry, writing in a recent issue of *Cross Currents,* says that in India, for example, as many as 100 million Indians are unemployed. "If Mr. Nehru's third Five Year Plan succeeds," Ferry writes, "it will produce another 10 million jobs. But an additional 15 million people will by then be waiting for them." The problem of an escalating technology is not so acute in America, *yet*, but we will have a population of 270 million six years from now, and the percentage of the permanently unemployed will go up rather than down. Many Americans can be retrained to take their places in the new automated society, but many are too old, and many do not have the basic education prerequisite to retraining for gainful employment in the space age. But these Americans have a right to continue to live, and with dignity.

We have a corresponding duty to share with them the benefits of the wondrous technology which has wrested from them the emancipating dignity of work. They are the victims of the historical flux. If this most advanced of all societies has kept them uneducated, unskilled, and unemployable, for whatever reason, or if it has not in times past provided realistic incentives for their development and improvement, then ultimately this society must share with them the profits accruing to the birthright of full citizenship they have had no chance to enjoy. In a world where people are starving for food no less than for the simple recognition of their humanity, and in a society where the imbalance of wealth between those who have and those who suffer from not having is extreme, the rationale for such a system becomes less discernible, and traditional attitudes about the sacredness and the inviolability of the capitalistic enterprise suffer the gravest erosion. The welfare state is not a reasonable alternative, for the welfare state destroys the soul while trying to salvage what is left of the body. Yet a sharply increased sense of responsibility—*social* responsibility, which, looking beyond the profit motive, can see *the people* brought to distress through instrumentalities they neither recognize nor understand—is imperative. We may no longer shut out the uncomfortable realities of hunger and crime and destitution by the simple device of averting the eyes or closing the mind, for they obtrude into consciousness with a persistence that accepts no further delay.

3. INTERNATIONAL PEACE

The experts list at least five kinds of accidents which could plunge the United States into nuclear war any hour of any day. First, a miscalculation or misinterpretation of an act by either the United States or Russia. Both the Russians and we have "trip-wire forces" set to unleash retaliatory missiles before an attack is experienced if it *appears* that the other side has mounted an attack. Secondly, the accidental detonation of a nuclear device (such as almost happened in North Carolina) is automatically detected by monitoring devices on both sides, but there is no way to tell whether the device was set off accidentally. If we think it was not an accident, we may attack. If the Russians think we think it was not an accident, they may attack in order to get in the first strike. If we think the Russians think that we think it was not an accident, we may attack so as to strike first. And so it goes. Thirdly, we could go to war "unintentionally" over a military incident that got out of hand, such as the holdup of one of our convoys on the autobahn into West Germany, or the escalation of a "local" situation like Vietnam or Cuba, or even Panama. Fourth, the "man-man" theory of accidental war is viable. While the key personnel controlling our weapons systems are carefully screened, even the most stable men have been known to break under the tensions associated with such dreadful responsibilities. Suppose Lee Harvey Oswald had been flying one of the nuclear-armed patrol bombers we keep constantly in the sky near the borders of Russia, or skipper of one of the many Polaris-bearing submarines we have probing the oceans of the world! A fifth type of accidental war may result from technological causes, the failure of a machine to correctly assess a given situation and make the right response.

These are ways in which war may come *by accident.* They do not take into consideration the constant presence of political frictions which could produce war by design. All things considered, we walk constantly on the edge of the abyss. There is no moment of our lives in which we have a reasonable assurance that it will be succeeded by another. The anxieties concomitant to such a state of continuing tension and uncertainty are robbing our lives of depth and meaning. As we come to accept the inevitability of destruction, we generate a value system consistent with this fact of existence. While we wish to live in peace, psychologically, we are perpetually involved in war, and we tend to live and express our lives as if life itself were vanity, a monstrous joke perpetrated upon a people doomed to die. We need a respite from the tension and anxieties of war. Our psychological orientation needs to be for peace. Fortunately, the era of the Big Two standing "eyeball to eyeball" with push buttons in hand seems to be declining. General U Thant, Secretary-General of the United Nations, believes that there are certain unmistakable trends toward new alignments in the world setup. "There have been fluctuations and vicissitudes in the fortunes of the big powers," he says. "My feeling is that in the seventies, if there are seventies, the world will witness four big powers, the United States of America, Europe, Russia, and China."

Such a happenstance will signal the decline of Russia and the United States to a position among equals—a rebalancing of power, which, if it does not make peace altogether impossible, will at least obviate the stand-off between the Russians and ourselves. Our respective peoples, the Russians and Americans, deserve a respite from the neurosis-producing anxieties that have so long characterized our relationship as the military sponsors of East versus West. Our President has made it clear to the Soviets that "we have no wish to bury anybody," and that we ourselves do not intend to be buried. Perhaps now, in 1964, we can go on with the matter of disengagement.

4. INTERNAL PEACE

The most crucial and sensitive problem confronting us today is internal peace. The internal peace of this country is predicated upon our ability to control reasonably the violent, right-wing extremism which is mushrooming in many of our towns and cities and to resolve equitably the racial issue, which threatens to become universal throughout the fifty states. At points these two social diseases come together in one foul malignancy, but for the most part they represent separate infections which we shall have to fight and fight hard.

The right-wing extremists like the Ku Klux Klan, the White Citizens Councils, the John Birch Society, the so-called Christian Crusades, and others of their ilk are all of a piece. Led by a handful of sinister ex-preachers, sick, retired generals, befuddled candy-makers, and discredited politicians, and followed, for the most part, by weak-minded men, frustrated housewives, and little old ladies in tennis shoes, their techniques are slanderous and undemocratic. Their stock-in-trade is hatred and suspicion; the ends they pursue are diabolical, and their danger to America is incalculable. They are the kind of people who did the screaming and clawing and cursing at Little Rock and New Orleans, who were serpentine enough to dare to spit on a man like Adlai Stevenson in Dallas, and who created the climate of hatred and lawlessness that made the assassination of our President a routine expectation.

The racial situation in this country is not encouraging. While some breakthroughs are registered here and there, the fundamental patterns of this racist society have changed but little. During 1963 there were 930 protest demonstrations in the South alone. Twenty thousand demonstrators were arrested. There were thirty-five bombings and ten people died under circumstances relating to racial protest. The savagery we saw in Birmingham was a distressing illustration of the bestial hatred characterizing the opposition to social change.

Change is inevitable, hatred or no hatred, blood or no blood. Nowhere in the world are intelligent men and women willing any longer to accept subjection to anybody on the flimsy and irrational premise that skin color makes some people better than others. The very idea is preposterous, and the people who believe it are either ignorant, sick, or both. It is past time for an enlightened America to discard these antiquated, egotistical, undemocratic patterns of thinking and get on with the business of making the full range of the common values of citizenship available to all our people. In the minds of twenty million determined Negro Americans, *discrimination is dead*. They have sought in every peaceful and reasonable way to communicate this idea to the bigots who keep the country in turmoil by setting themselves up as the racial arbiters of the public conscience. But only concerned Americans can make America truly democratic, and only responsible Americans can bring justice and order to this unjust and disordered society. Let America make haste! It is considerably later than we think. It has been said that the condition of the American Negro is today's bitterest joke about freedom and justice. Well, Negroes stopped laughing a long time ago, or hasn't anybody noticed?

PATTERNS OF PROTEST*

A protest movement is a symptom of a pervasive social conflict distorting the normal social relations between groups of people. It is an expression of the deep anxiety and discontent of one group reacting against what is perceived as the abuse of power by some other group. Power is the control over decisions. A protest movement is a reaction protesting that control or the character of its expression.

Direct action protest has become an important means of communicating the American Negro's extreme dissatisfaction with his condition of existence in America. But in spite of persistent protest, the racial situation is still not encouraging. In the fateful year of 1963 there were thirty-five bombings of homes and churches, and ten people died under circumstances relating to racial protest. The Federal Bureau of Investigation, which is highly touted for efficiency in bringing to justice criminals of every other sort and stripe, has been peculiarly ineffective in ferreting out and making effective cases against murderers and other malefactors whose crimes are against Negroes active in the civil rights movement. As a consequence the FBI, like some other institutions associated with law and order and justice, is in grave danger of losing the confidence

* Published in *The Christian Century*, June 3, 1964.

of Negroes who may come to see it as one more example on the long and weary list of institutionalized discrimination. Against a background of public passivity and official resistance to change, overt protest has been the Negro's most dramatic weapon for claiming for himself *now* rights that enhance his sense of dignity and self-respect. It is not his only weapon, nor is it necessarily his most effective one in the long run. But it does get the attention of those to whom the message is directed.

In the past year there have been at least 930 protest demonstrations in the South alone. Twenty thousand demonstrators were arrested, most of them from the militant and determined student organizations. Scores of Negroes were bitten by police dogs, pummeled by high-pressure hoses, and beaten by policemen as they sought to make known their grievances through peaceful and non-violent means. The summer ahead may be infinitely more tragic. Malcolm X, the Black Muslim racist, has urged publicly that Negroes organize rifle clubs to protect themselves. Few Negroes want violence, but there is a growing consensus that uncontrolled violence could erupt if police brutality persists, or if Negroes are not protected from the clubs, bombs, and rifles of white racists.

I

Racial protest is not new, of course. As an aggressive expression of a subordinated group, or as a challenge to the morality and justice of the abuse of power, protest has been practiced in various forms by Negroes since they were first brought to America as slaves. The forms of protest have been many—and not always nonviolent. From arson to armed insurrection and from infanticide to suicide, the Negro has sought by whatever means available to him to make known his objection to the white man's concept of his "place" in the

American scheme of things. The white man's characteristic response has been a studied obliviousness. The traditional arrangement of hegemony and subordination has not changed. There have been "adjustments" within the system, but the system itself has remained substantially intact. The Negro has been damned by the myth of white supremacy. But it is difficult to sell a new myth in the face of one so long established and so formidably entrenched.

The present status of Negro-white relations is an inevitable phase in the progressive displacement of the slave image and the eventual fulfillment of the implications of true citizenship in a democratic society. The initial structure of white-black relationships was that of master and slave. The posture of the master was proprietary. He *owned* whatever there was in the slave that could be reduced to property values and protected by law. The response of the slave was resignation. It was not an abject acceptance; rather, it was resignation in the face of the insuperable power of the American state, the unfavorable geographic conditions which placed the slave on a strange continent an ocean away from home and help, the monolithic character of tradition and opinion in the South, and such institutions as law, economics, and religion, all of which supported slavery.

It is probably not an overstatement to say that the slave never did accept fully his role in the social order; this was demonstrated by his continuing protests. But it became clear to him that the odds were too great for *effective* protest and he prudently resigned himself to a period of servitude. His only real options were slavery or death, and although thousands chose death the vast majority elected to live for the day when the odds against their freedom would be less conclusive.

In short, the slave resigned himself to what he could not change, but he did not accept his status as moral, inevitable, or permanent. The slave communicated his expectation of deliverance in his spirituals and his folk tales. The white man heard what the slave was saying, but because of his own arrogance and his irrevocable commitment to a slave economy he was unable to make a moral response. To the white man the freedom and the equality of the slave were inconceivable categories. There was no meeting of minds between him and his slave, and it is probable that no true communication between races took place on a significant scale until quite recent times.

II

The next relationship in the progression was the citizen and freedman. The Emancipation Proclamation, the successful conclusion of the Civil War, and the enactment of the Thirteenth Amendment together brought freedom to all the Negroes in bondage. The Fourteenth Amendment purported to make citizens of them, and the Fifteenth Amendment conferred upon them the right to vote. But the right to vote did little to enhance the freedmen's status as citizens. Even during the Reconstruction period the franchise did not establish social and political equivalence for the erstwhile slaves, nor did it bring to them the economic security which might have permitted a more effective exercise of the citizenship they thought they had. In less than a generation even the Negro's right to vote was challenged throughout the South, and although he retained that right as an abstract principle of constitutional law, the opportunity to exercise it was scarcely afforded him after 1878.

Hence the Negro's citizenship was defective from the beginning, and this fact has important overtones in his present relationship to the white man. In the mind of the white man, the Negro is simply different. The universal laws, traditions, and social attitudes which have characteristically operated to protect and guarantee the preeminence of citizens in their own country have never in the history of America fully included the Negro. As a matter of fact, the "citizenship" of every Negro has generally availed him less protection and respect than has the white skin of any foreigner traveling or residing in this democratic commonwealth!

The political relationship between whites and Negroes since Reconstruction has been popularly referred to as a relationship between citizens and "second-class" citizens. But second-class citizenship has no meaning. At best it is a euphemism for the political limbo between slavery and citizenship. In his social relations with the white man the Negro assumed a role of accommodation, and as is characteristic of accommodative relationships, communication remained restricted and essentially ceremonial. The white man "heard" only what was consistent with the ideological presuppositions of white supremacy. The Negro accommodated himself to the white man's self-image by reciting to the white man the words the white man had taught him to say and wished him to believe. Obviously there was no viable communication; no transfer of ideas took place. The white man went on believing what he heard the Negro say, and it was expedient for the Negro to go on saying what the white man wanted to believe.

There was protest, to be sure, but real communication was negated for two principal reasons: (1) The Negro spoke from weakness rather than from strength, and the white man's response was paternalistic rather than equalitarian. (2) Where the Negro dared to be assertive rather than supplicative, he did not speak directly to the white man but to his institutions, i.e., to the legal, religious, and economic entities which stand between the white man and the consequences of his behavior.

Direct action techniques—sit-ins, protest marches, selective buying, etc.—have ushered in a new category of relationship. Communication between the races has never been better than it is today. The widespread lamentations over the alleged

"breakdown of communications" between the races in the
South result from a very grievous misinterpretation of what
is involved in social communication. What is actually being
lamented is the demise of a superficial "cordiality" which illustrated our ceremonial approach to the idea, albeit unwittingly,
that the white man "knows the Negro"—what he wants, what
he needs, and how he will behave under specialized circumstances. This dogma is a product of racial paternalism and
segregationist ideology. The white man does not "know" the
Negro, has never known him, and has never seriously undertaken to find out what the Negro is like as a person. It is
patent that in a caste society members of the upper caste are
manifestly prohibited by caste proscriptions from the kind of
contact and interchange of ideas which would enable them to
"know" members of the lower caste. For most of the history
of biracial America the white man has considered the Negro
to be a different order of being altogether—another species of
animal, scarcely capable of the white man's idealized moral
and cultural pretensions. This fundamental absurdity alone
constituted a firm barrier to an intelligent assessment of the
Negro as a human being.

There has been no breakdown in communication because
responsible communication between the races did not exist
until the Negro abandoned the ceremonies of the old arrangement and began speaking directly to the white man, expressing
his true feelings and underscoring his attitudes with overt,
illustrative behavior. The white man's response has often been
one of bewilderment, chagrin, and fear. He is bewildered
because he has come to believe his own indoctrination. He
honestly thought he knew the Negro. What he really knew
was the image of the Negro that he himself had created. His
chagrin stems from self-delusion, and his fear and anxiety are
natural products of being caught off guard at a crucial moment in history. For the first time he is listening to what the

Negro is trying to tell him—and he is required by circumstances to make a nonperfunctory response.

III

We have reached a healthy impasse. The white man's deliberate ignorance of the Negro as a person and of his aspirations as a citizen has been overcome. From this point forward the only alternatives to the practice of equality will be the expulsion of the Negro or his annihilation. Since such extreme alternatives are not viable in a democracy, it is inevitable that a reconstruction in race relations is at hand. Negroes will be "legal equals" and will be treated as such. The expression of the democratic ideal will at least approximate the spirit and intent of the law.

The true equalitarian society is somewhat more distant. Because an enlightened society always sets its highest moral values beyond its legal expectations, the millennium cannot come with the mere observance of legal justice. Legal justice is a significant attainment in the maturation of a society. It assures that every man will receive what is his due, thereby assuring the equality of citizens before the law. But legal justice and social morality are not necessarily the same thing, and at this point in our development neither the white man nor his black counterpart has attained the moral maturity that looks very far beyond legal justice. Indeed, we are but now approaching the threshold from which we may contemplate seriously the simple legal axiom of rendering to every man his due.

The new communication which has evolved between blacks and whites has not come without bitterness and hostility. Thousands of Negroes who have been engaged in communicating with the white man through direct action have been brutally assaulted. In Birmingham fire hoses and vicious dogs were turned upon Negro demonstrators who wanted no more than to make known their attitudes toward segregation. In Jackson, Mississippi, convicts were used to throw scores of Negroes into foul-smelling garbage trucks to be hauled off to makeshift compounds like so many swine. The crime which brought about so brutish an attempt at humiliation was the Negro's peaceful protest against discrimination. *The irony of it all is that the Negroes confronting the white man today refuse to be humiliated.* In Jackson they accepted the garbage trucks and prayed for the white men who preferred to abuse them rather than to hear what they had to say about freedom. They were trying to convey to the white people of Jackson that in the minds of the Negro masses segregation is more contemptible than a ride in a garbage truck. The racial dialogue can be dangerous; some Negroes engaged in it have been murdered, and the number of killings will probably continue to mount as the situation becomes more acute.

"Moderates" in both racial camps tend to be more concerned over whether Negroes and whites "hate" each other than they are over the resolution of the issues. This concern reflects a genuine passion for the common realization of the moral values implicit in the American creed. To the "moderate" it does not seem rational that in an advanced Christian democracy citizens who have worked together, fought together, worshiped the same God (albeit in separate congregations!), and known each other so intimately for so many generations could suddenly have developed a consuming hatred for each other. Of course, the presuppositions of any who think in these terms are faulty to begin with. Our racial "togetherness" has been essentially fictional. We have worked, fought, and even lived *side by side,* but seldom "together." We have indeed worshiped the same God, but our prayers and expectations have been based on different perspectives.

IV

The unhappy truth is that hatred is an integral part of any caste society, and the more strict the observance of the forms which hold the system together, the more intense the hatred is likely to be. It is inevitable that the intense hostility and resentment accumulated through generations of preserving (or attacking) the American caste system will find expression in increasing violence. The alternative is the development of measures to accomplish rapid desegregation which obviate direct and hostile confrontation between blacks and whites who have disparate values at stake.

Social conflict within a consensual framework may be functional of course, for consensus precludes the emergency of the uncontrolled violence which ignores the rules and the weapons of the consensus. Where consensus is not present, conflict may be extremely dysfunctional. The danger in relying on direct action techniques, for example, lies in the possibility of assuming consensus where there is none. This is what precipitated the riot in Birmingham. The "rules" of the protest demonstrations had been clearly established in scores of sit-ins and wade-ins and prayer marches throughout the South over the past several years. Each racial faction in Birmingham knew what the other expected of it. The intentions of the demonstrators were prominently announced in the press and through radio and television. But there was no consensus. The white police descended upon the marchers with dogs and fire hoses. White hoodlums bombed homes and businesses in the Negro community. The Negroes responded with assaults upon white persons, and with burning and pillaging. None of these activities was within the rules of consensus.

There is no reason to believe that more serious violence will not erupt in the absence of positive measures on the part of the federal government or some other agency capable of emancipating the Negro from the shackles of prejudice and discrimination. The proliferation of "nonviolent" attacks on Southern institutions has resulted in a situation of increasing anxiety for the Southern white man who perceives them as a threat to the values he has identified with life itself. But the Negro's anxieties increase too, for the nearer he approaches his goal, the more elusive it seems to become.

As more whites are able to break with the undemocratic ways of thinking and acting which characterized the relationships between the races in the past, and as more Negroes are admitted to the enjoyment of the common values of citizenship, racism as a philosophy will decline, as will the hatred endemic to our caste system. There is already some evidence that many white people, including some Southerners, are daring to see some Negroes as being essentially like themselves. This is a healthy sign for America. Some whites and some Negroes will never overcome their racial hatred, since a need to feel superior is integral to their basic personality structures. Some well-meaning moderates would solve the problem by turning the South into another North. God forbid. That is not the answer. The only lasting solution is complete equalitarianism, the equalitarianism that gives a man the right to be black or white or any other color and still enjoy the full benefits of citizenship. Now that Negroes and whites have begun talking to each other on a serious level, that which has been a dream for so many generations may become a reality tomorrow.

KEY MAN OF THE SOUTH—
THE NEGRO MINISTER*

One of the most maligned institutions in America has been the Negro church, one of the most caricatured professions the Negro ministry. Today, however, the Negro minister is teaching America to perceive him in a new light. The civil rights movement at the grass-roots level is largely in the hands of ministers, and the ministers themselves have found a new dignity which lifts them above the stereotype of pompous behavior, fried chicken, and expensive automobiles with which they were once identified.

The Negro minister has had to come a long way. During the slave period, Negro ministers were rare, for any form of black leadership was considered inimical to the interests of the slavocracy. At first slaves were admitted to the galleries of white churches; later it was not unusual for white preachers to preach carefully selected sermons to gatherings of slaves. In a few places Negro exhorters or self-styled preachers were permitted to hold services in the presence of the white overseer or some other white man designated to monitor the meetings.

However, most religious services led by early Negro

* Published in *The New York Times Magazine*, July 12, 1964.

preachers were clandestine, held deep in the swamps and forests to escape detection. It was at such secret meetings that the "freedom spirituals" denying the permanency of slavery, and promising deliverance by a just and avenging God, were developed. It was here, too, that the dual role of the Negro preacher as a spiritual leader and as a protest leader was first developed.

Freedom from bondage brought with it the freedom to choose a profession, at least theoretically, and the ministry was the profession most readily available to Negro men. Between the end of the Civil War and the turn of the twentieth century, certainly more Negroes went into the ministry than into any other profession.

Until fairly recently it was required only that a preacher "know his Bible" better than his congregation and be able to preach and pray in an "arousing" manner in order to found or lead a church. Frequently the first requirement was readily waived if a man could "preach the Word with force and conviction" and set the congregation to "shouting" with his imagery and showmanship. God would tell him what to say, as he told Moses in Egypt and countless other prophets in Hebrew history.

Booker T. Washington was fond of telling the story of a Negro farmer who was plowing in the field one day when he suddenly exclaimed: "Lord, this sun is so hot, this grass is so tall and this doggone mule is so stubborn, I b'lieve I hear you calling me to preach!" With that he left mule and plow standing in the field and went off to found a church.

Free-wheeling preaching begot a free-wheeling response like that in a Baptist church I knew as a boy in north Alabama. Every Sunday night Aunt Sally Rogers (who was older than any could remember) would "get happy" and "walk the benches"; this frail little woman of ninety pounds or so would climb to the backs of the pews and walk them rigidly from the rear to the front of the church and back again, singing and shouting and flinging aside those who got in her way.

Down in front of those churches of a generation or so ago was the "moaners' bench," where confessed sinners sat through the long revival meetings hoping to be touched by the Spirit and cleansed of their sins. Amid much preaching and singing, praying and shouting, the sinners were usually delivered of their burdens, and with shouts of ecstasy and tears of joy on all sides they were received into the fellowship of the church.

Probably every Negro who grew up in the South before the last World War knows from personal experience the meaning of the knotted handkerchief. Women like my grandmother would tie a quarter in one corner of their Sunday handkerchief for church dues and fifteen cents in the opposite corner for burial insurance. And nothing on earth save "good preaching" and good singing at the village church could unknot the twenty-five-cent end of that handkerchief. Occasionally at the Sunday-night services my grandmother would even put her "insurance money" into the collection plate and "trust the Lord to take care of her" until she could catch up on her insurance. But the insurance man never got what belonged to the church.

The Negro's preoccupation with church dues and insurance was, of course, a reflection of the precarious circumstances in which he lived. As late as 1940, the total income of many Southern Negro families did not exceed five or six dollars a week, very often considerably less. As a consequence, the emphasis of the living was directed largely toward preparation for dying, and in this preparation the minister played a part of great importance. Faithful membership in his church would assure a better life "over Jordan."

But the minister was deeply concerned with his members' lives this side of Jordan too. Despite his professional shortcomings and his frequent inclination to make the church organizations instrumental to his personal aggrandizement, he was the most important leader in the community, and sometimes the only one. The Negro community looked to him as their spokesman before the mysterious white world and trusted him to keep their affairs in order.

Today the number of Negroes entering the ministry is diminishing in relation to other professional interest (although, except for teaching, it probably remains the largest single profession among Negroes). At the same time the quality of this training is fast improving. Dr. Harry Richardson, president of Atlanta's Interdenominational Theological Center, the largest predominantly Negro seminary in the country, says that "Negro youth are now deliberately choosing the ministry rather than being pushed into it by lack of opportunity in other fields." In some Negro denominations today the minister must have at least a college degree, with further training in a seminary—although this rule is far from universal and most Negro pastors are still concentrated in denominations where a minister need only be "called of God" in order to preach.

The "typical" Southern Negro minister is probably as elusive as the "typical" anything else, but in order to take a closer look at the role of the contemporary Negro minister in the South, I followed the Reverend A. S. Dickerson through his ministerial paces for several days. Mr. Dickerson, whose given names are Adolphus Sumner, is pastor of Central Methodist Church in Atlanta. His church has about 1,500 members and is located in an urban-renewal area near downtown Atlanta.

Pastor Dickerson is fifty years old and was born in a small town in western Georgia. Ordained in 1937, he has advanced until he is now head of one of the largest churches in his conference. He holds or has held many important positions on the various boards or committees of his conference, and has had a term on the trustee board of a church-related Negro college in Atlanta, a few blocks from his church. Mr. Dickerson is better educated than most Negro ministers, holding advanced degrees from Atlanta University and Boston University. He met his wife, Virginia, in "church work," and they own their own home.

Two services are held each Sunday morning at Central Methodist Church, one at 8:15 and another at 10:45. Mr. Dickerson's assistant, the Reverend W. H. McIver, officiates at the early service. I attended the 10:45 service on two successive Sundays, and both times the sanctuary was almost filled, with 400 or 500 worshipers. Some of the women wore furs and jewelry. Others dressed quite plainly. I learned later that many of the older members who moved away after the neighborhood began deteriorating still come back for Sunday services, although they are less active in week-night activities.

The church service was more or less routine, the order of worship being taken from the *Official Methodist Hymnal.* The sermon preached on my first visit, "The Will to Overcome," was forcefully presented, yet with a certain dignity and restraint. On this visit there was no "shouting" or weeping. However, on the next Sunday during Communion, as the congregation began to sing "Let Us Break Bread Together," a large woman in the choir became overwrought and began to scream and wave her arms. She was restrained, but only after her outburst had started a chain reaction of shouts and sobbing throughout the church.

In some class-conscious Negro churches it is no longer "acceptable" to "shout." I asked Mr. Dickerson whether "shouting" occurred frequently in his church. He said that the practice, while acceptable, was diminishing.

Following his sermon, Pastor Dickerson talked briefly with his congregation about civic issues and their responsibilities as citizens. Two items claimed his attention in particular. One was the necessity of restraint and nonviolence in the continuing fight for first-class citizenship. "First-class citizenship we *must* have and we *will* have," he asserted, "but not at the expense of law and order."

The second item was a coming referendum to decide whether Atlanta was to make the sale of mixed drinks legal, or whether liquor sales would be restricted to package stores. Of this he said, "The way you vote is your business, isn't it? That is the American way. But *do vote*, and vote responsibly! It is your duty. If you want to be citizens, you must exercise the responsibilities of citizens."

Mr. Dickerson's week is hectic. He is a part-time chaplain at the Atlanta Federal Penitentiary, and on Monday I accompanied him there. As we made our way to the chaplain's office he was sought out by a succession of prisoners who wanted variously to share a joke with him, make an appointment, or just shake hands. All the prisoners who sought to speak with him that day were white.

Next day Mr. Dickerson was one of a handful of Negro ministers and educators asked to meet with members of the Emory University Medical School faculty to discuss ways of improving the health of indigent mothers and their children. Some of the ministers present suspected a ruse to make birth control mandatory for Negro mothers (who constitute about 80 per cent of the indigent cases). Mr. Dickerson thought no, but he suggested that any board selected to oversee the matter, and the team of doctors who would administer any proposed program, should have "effective representation" from Negro professionals from the beginning.

Tuesday night there was choir rehearsal. Central Methodist has only two choirs, although some Negro churches have as many as six or seven, for the numerous choirs not only provide a popular outlet for church participation, but they compete with each other in raising money to augment the church treasury. On Wednesday night there was a Midweek Prayer Meeting, the Young Adult Fellowship, and a rehearsal of the Senior Choir.

Thursday afternoon I went calling with Pastor Dickerson for a glimpse of the people who would make up his parish and their ways of life. One call took us to the home of an elderly widow a block or two from the church. On the way Mr. Dickerson explained that he did not ordinarly telephone before calling, as he did not like his parishioners to feel special preparations were necessary for a visit from the pastor.

The widow was obviously pleased to receive us. In a room filled with old clocks, pictures, statuary, and bric-a-brac from bygone times, she waved me to a chair half hidden under a profusion of old magazines and newspapers. She and Mr. Dickerson shared an ancient piano bench.

"Reverend," she exclaimed, recovering from her surprise, and trying valiantly to conceal a wad of snuff in her bottom lip, "Reverend, I *knowed* you were coming to see me! My rheumatism's been bothering me so, and that ol' landlord done been acting so mean—threatening to put me out and all—I just had a feeling that you were coming to see me! Bless the Lord, you don't forget me!"

The minister listened patiently to her troubles and, before leaving, offered prayer. As we stood up to go, from somewhere in the folds of her ancient gingham, the old lady produced a handkerchief carefully knotted at opposite corners. "Reverend," she said quietly as she fumbled with one of the knots, "if I don't make it to church Sunday, I want you to have my dues." She unfolded two worn one-dollar bills and handed them to her pastor.

Another call was at the home of a prominent businessman in a meticulously kept neighborhood which had been the showplace of black Atlanta fifteen years ago. The spacious homes were set discreetly back from the gracefully curving street on which they bordered. The dogwoods and azaleas offered a variety of color, and the lush green lawns were neatly clipped. We stopped before a large ranch house which easily dominated the street. The front door was open, but no one answered the bell. The pastor left his card.

Friday night is "Fun Night" at the Central Methodist Church, providing an opportunity for the minister to meet the young people of his congregation in a relaxed atmosphere. There are games and group singing and refreshments, but no dancing. Adults attend Fun Night, too, and the pastor enters enthusiastically into the spirit of the evening.

On Saturday Mr. Dickerson prepares his sermon and "tries to do a little reading and meditation." In his busy week he manages to find time for a full share of civic responsibilities, to teach a class at the Interdenominational Theological Center, and to carry a fairly heavy counseling load, lending a hand to those in trouble whether or not they belong to his church.

"My people, like all people, have problems," he reflected. "Families are broken, teenagers get into trouble, somebody's furniture is set out on the street. I have to go and do what I can do to help them. This is my job. I wouldn't change it."

Like almost every other effective Negro minister in the South today, Mr. Dickerson is active in the civil rights movement, although he does not consider himself to be a "professional" civil rights leader. A few months ago when Negro leadership in Atlanta met in a series of day-long "summit conferences" to formulate means of coordinating an attack on remaining segregation in Atlanta, he was prominently involved, although he shies from publicity.

"Whenever it is possible," he explained, "I prefer to meet the white man in quiet negotiation. I do not mean that we should talk merely for the sake of talking. Conversation is not a reasonable substitute for action. But we should go into the streets only as a last resort, and once there we should conduct ourselves reasonably; but we ought to be prepared to stay until the job is done. Above all things, we should remember that the white man, too, is a personality, a personality we no more wish to destroy than to have our own personalities destroyed."

Here Dickerson represents a growing feeling among responsible Negro clergymen that the Negro minister must assume some responsibility for protecting society from the consequences of the white man's bias and helping the white man toward a kind of self-reclamation.

In Atlanta there is a strong Republican tradition among Negroes, and they have labored tirelessly for a two-party system in Georgia. Mr. Dickerson has no political ambitions of his own, but he works hard in the Fulton County Republican Club, "not just for the sake of party partisanship, but in order that all our people may be freed eventually from the tyranny of a single party."

His colleagues in the ministry hold Pastor Dickerson in high respect, as does the white establishment with which he is in constant contact. It is not a patronizing attitude with the latter. Warden David Heritage of the Atlanta Federal Penitentiary called Dickerson "as able a chaplain as I have seen without regard to race. And a good man." When Mr. Dickerson was named chairman of a grievance committee dealing with a civil rights issue, a Negro service-station attendant said: "I ain't a-tall worried. So long as Reverend Dickerson is going to be the one to talk to them white folks, you don't have to worry about getting sold out."

There are still Negro ministers in the South and elsewhere who belong to the stereotype of ill-prepared, money-grubbing, chicken-eating, women-chasing, gold-toothed frauds, but they are, as I have said, a vanishing breed. Here and there a Baptist congregation still shows its "appreciation" of its minister by giving him a new Cadillac and a "love offering"

of several thousand dollars a year, but such behavior is fast
becoming obsolete.

When the Negro's only sense of prestige and dignity was
derived vicariously through the person and status of his minister, it was understandable and perhaps even pardonable.
When Negroes were hungry, they fed the preacher; when
ragged, they clothed him with expensive suits; while they
walked, they bought the pastor a big car.

But times have changed. Every man is now in search of his
own dignity, and he expects his minister to lead him to finding it. Those unprepared to lead are on their way out.

THE NEGRO'S
MIDDLE-CLASS DREAM*

A famous professor at a large university used to begin one of his lectures in social psychology with a description of the characteristics of a typical American family. After he had described the family's income, address, religion, the kind of car they drove, organizations to which they belonged, and the occupation of the father, he would then demand to know what social class the family belonged to. But before the students could answer, the professor would add as an apparent afterthought: "Oh yes, I forgot to mention that this is a *Negro* family!" Inevitably the students were stymied. What had begun as a simple problem became insolubly complex by the addition of the word "Negro."

Where do Negroes fit into the prevailing American class structure? Most sociologists say they don't. Negroes have a *parallel* social structure, somewhat—but not entirely—analogous to that of whites. This social parallelism, or two-caste society, is created by the color barrier which, with the rarest exceptions, prevents lateral movement from class to class between Negroes and whites. As a prominent Negro matron said in Detroit, "We Negroes and whites visit each other at times, and frequently we belong to the same civic organiza-

* Published in *The New York Times Magazine*, October 25, 1964.

133

tions and attend the same functions, but the lines are there, and no one has to say where they are."

The Negro class structure had its roots in the institution of American slavery, which, in ignoring the African's cultural presumptions, leveled all classes and force-fused highly disparate individuals and groups into one conglomerate mass—"the Negro slave," or simply "the Negro," a word which, in America, became synonymous with "slave" or the "descendant of slaves." Prince and servant, Eboe and Mandingo, Moslem and spirit-worshiper were all the same to the slavemaster, who saw them only as commodities to be bought and sold, or as a labor supply for his vast plantations.

Whatever the basis of past distinctions, the Negro social structure in America had to evolve out of conditions connected with plantation life, and within a context which recognized the absolute superiority of the white slave owner (although not necessarily that of the small, non-slaveholding white farmers, who were looked upon by house servants and slave owners alike as "poor white trash").

The Negro's "society," then, had four more or less distinct social classes. In ascending order, they were: (1) field hands (who had least contact with the socializing influences of the white environment); (2) mechanics and artisans (bricklayers, carpenters, ironworkers, bakers, etc., who were frequently hired out by the month or the year to merchants or builders in the cities); (3) valets, butlers, maids, cooks, and other household servants (whose frequent personal contact with whites made them the most "acculturated" class), and (4) free Negroes (who had bought their freedom or had become free by manumission—often because of faithfulness or some heroic exploit).

As slaves, the house-servant class had by far the highest proportion of mulattoes. While this did not by any means exempt them from the normal rigors incident to being slaves, including sale, the light-skinned mistresses of the slavemasters were often granted petty privileges and their children were more frequently given their freedom than those of any other class.

At the end of the slave period the mulattoes sought to establish themselves as a distinct occupational and social class within the Negro subculture. For the most part they continued as servants and retainers to their erstwhile masters—as dressmakers, barbers, coachmen, and the like. For more than a generation they clung tenaciously to a certain degree of status derived from catering exclusively to the "quality" folk (as they had done in slavery) under the then current slogan of (serving) "mighty few white folks and no niggers a-tall!"

By the turn of the century, however, as the economy of the South began to revive, the mulatto "retainers" were progressively displaced by European immigrants and poor whites who were suddenly willing to do "Negro work." From that date neither occupation nor color has been a reliable index of social standing among Negroes.

Today a light skin is not an automatic key to social status. In this day of the Negro's increasing race pride and his subtle impulse to nationalism, a light skin *can* be a handicap, especially if it is associated with "recent" miscegenation. Mass education and the indiscriminate rise to power and money of significant numbers of Negroes irrespective of their grandparents' station in the slave society have all but destroyed the effectiveness of the Negro's private color bar. Leadership in civil rights as well as in the professions has long since passed from the mulatto class. As a matter of fact, the number of mulattoes in the general Negro population seems to be declining steadily and there is no evidence that legal integration will soon replace clandestine miscegenation in restoring the ratio of light color.

There is no unanimity of opinion as to what proportion of

today's Negroes fall into the traditional "lower," "middle," and "upper" classes of the Negro social structure. Prof. Tillman Cothran, head of the graduate department of sociology at Atlanta University, estimates that "not more than 25 per cent of the Negro population can be called middle class by any reasonable standards. And not more than 5 per cent can be called upper class."

Other sociologists have argued that if one applies the full spectrum of criteria by which the white social structure is measured—ranging from income to education, affiliation, residence, etc.—the Negro middle class is reduced to 4 per cent or 5 per cent of the Negro population, and the Negro upper class vanishes altogether.

Such an estimate is, I think, too drastic. If the theory of parallel social structure is valid (and there seems to be no other way to measure "class" in an essentially segregated society), certainly it can be shown that Negroes and whites of similar education and income exhibit many of the same desires, restraints, conformities, and general patterns of behavior.

America's self-image is that of an essentially equalitarian society best represented by the middle class. Most Americans concede that there are a few snobs and millionaires at the top, and a few poor people in Appalachia, or somewhere, at the bottom, but America is middle-class, and most Americans identify themselves as belonging to the middle class.

Implicit in this identification is a belief in "democracy" and "fair play," and also the expectation of "the good life"—a home, a car, a regular vacation, an education for the children, regular promotions, and maybe even extras like a boat or a summer place. Despite the pessimism of the sociologists, more and more Negroes share this dream, and to an increasing degree they are making it come true for themselves and their children.

The Negro middle class is made up primarily of Negro professionals, with schoolteachers probably constituting the largest single bloc. Teachers along with doctors, lawyers, college professors, small businessmen, ministers, and postal workers have traditionally made up the bulk of the Negro middle class.

However, the recent availability of new kinds of jobs not previously held by Negroes has begun to modify the character of this group. Technicians, politicians, clerical and sales personnel, social workers, labor-union officials, minor government bureaucrats, and an increasing managerial class in such agencies as federal housing and local units of national corporations have helped to broaden the occupational range of the Negro middle class.

Under the Kennedy-Johnson Administration a few Negroes have been appointed to the upper echelons of government officialdom, and within the past two or three years a few Negroes have reached executive status in white corporations. A recent dinner in New York honored seven Negroes who were vice-presidents or held managerial positions in major firms. In Washington, Dr. James Nabrit, President of Howard University, and Dr. Frank Jones have been elected to the board of directors of a major bank. And in that city several Negroes have been elected to the Board of Trade.

It is difficult to set a salary range for a given social class because social status does not depend on money alone. Some upper-class whites are impoverished, but their families have once held fortunes and they have traditions of culture and attainment. Since the American Negro's family traditions seldom antedate the Civil War, Negro society puts an undue emphasis on money and material acquisitions. It is often said by Negro critics themselves that "anybody with a dollar, no matter where he stole it, can belong to Negro society."

Most Negroes, like most other Americans, earn their living legitimately, of course, but because of job discrimination and lack of skills, the total income of the typical middle-class Negro family will be substantially lower than that of a typical white family of the middle class. An arbitrary figure of $7,500 a year as the average income of a middle-class family would severely limit the number of Negroes who could be called middle-class.

Some Negro families do exceed a $7,500 income, but the vast majority of those who do are families in which both husband and wife work full time. Very frequently among home-buying Negroes, the head of the family works at two jobs, and occasionally at three. Such supplementary work or "moonlighting"—often driving a taxi, waiting on tables, tending bar, or bell-hopping—is known as "a hustle," a term quite familiar to the Negro middle class.

In many of the large cities of the North such as New York or Boston where undeveloped land is nonexistent, the middle-class Negro, who has the means and the desire to live else-where, is locked in the black ghetto. Only with difficulty can he find a house or apartment outside the ghetto in a white community. As a consequence, many Negroes despair of ever leaving the slums, no matter what their education or income.

Money that would normally go for a new house is spent in the hopeless task of refurbishing antiquated apartments, or in conspicuous consumption which somehow helps them to forget the horror of living in the nation's Harlems. (In the South the housing problem is not nearly so acute. Space for building can be had in most Southern cities, although it is likely to be in a segregated community.)

The style of living of the Negro middle class does not differ radically from that of its white counterpart. Bridge is a favorite pastime among both men and women. Those who have the leisure belong to innumerable social clubs. An increasing number of Negro men play golf and participate in water sports where facilities are available. In the South fishing and hunting are favorite pastimes, but only if one has the full regalia of dress and all the latest equipment shown in the sports magazines.

To a far greater degree than whites, Negroes maintain affiliation in the graduate chapters of their college fraternities and sororities, and these organizations are important indexes of social stratification. Women of a given sorority tend to marry men of its fraternal opposite number. Together the eight major Negro sororities and fraternities constitute the nucleus of any imaginary "blue book" of Negro society.

The children of the Negro middle class are taught to aspire to middle-class standards. They take lessons in piano and creative dancing on Saturday mornings and attend carefully planned parties on Saturday night. A few are sent East to private schools.

Sometimes the interpretation of middle-class values takes an unusual twist. A Negro matron in a Memphis department store, for example, refused to corral her two children who were busily chasing through the store and littering the aisles with merchandise. She explained: "The white kids do it and the salesclerks think it's cute. I don't want my children inhibited by feeling that they can't do anything any other kids can do."

In Washington, among those aspiring to the middle class, or those who are recently "in," status is measured by the quantity and the cost of whiskey served one's guests. The most conspicuous feature in such a home will be the bar appointments, and it is considered equally insulting for a guest to refuse a drink as it is for the host to offer his guests "cheap whiskey." One Washingtonian gained prominence in his set by consistently being first to serve rare and expensive imports before they were well known in the Negro community. He learned what was "in" by frequenting an exclusive liquor store patronized by high government officials.

It used to be said that the difference between a Negro mak-

ing $50 a week and driving a Cadillac and a white man making
$100 a week and driving a Chevrolet was that the Negro,
having nowhere to live, needed the bigger car to sleep in! On
Atlanta's West Side, where the Cadillac (or Lincoln) frequently comes with a split-level ranch house, it is popular to
have the main (or "status") car match the house in color and
appointments.

A second car for the Negro professional family is not unusual. Unlike most white middle-class families having two
cars, the Negro's second car is likely to be as big and expensive as his first. An expensive automobile to drive to work is
often as much a matter of personal prestige for the working
Negro woman as for her husband. Hence, it is common to see
large numbers of Pontiacs, Oldsmobiles, and Mercurys parked
near the schools where Negro women are employed as teachers.

A cottage at Oak Bluffs, on Martha's Vineyard, or in Maine
or Upper Michigan can be claimed by a few. A very small
number of Negroes go to Europe and to the Caribbean or
Mexico on vacation. A sort of pilgrimage of Africa has high
status value for those seeking to "understand their pre-West-
ern heritage."

Some Negroes are in the middle class because there is nowhere else for them to go. These few might be considered
"upper class," but there is a certain incongruity in talking about
a Negro "upper class" so long as the color barrier operates
to bar Negroes who are otherwise qualified from full participation in American social life. "There may not be an upper
class," says Clarence Coleman, southeastern director of the
National Urban League, "but there is a 'power elite' which
abstracts itself from the rank and file of the middle class and
participates to an important extent in the decision-making of
the white power structure where Negroes are concerned."

Certainly this power elite does exist. But where it was not
created by the white establishment, its power derives from

white recognition and respect. Militant civil rights leaders have discovered this again and again when the white establishment has refused to negotiate with the Negro community except through "recognized channels."

The Negro middle class, like any middle class, is preoccupied with making secure its hard-won social position. This is a characteristic of middle-class aspirations.

Because of this preoccupation the Negro middle class has been criticized for not being more deeply and realistically involved in the struggle for civil rights. The criticism is well placed, for given more manpower, more money, and more dedication, it is obvious that more walls could be breached. But this is not the whole story, and the lack of total involvement may not be an accurate index of middle-class feelings and intentions.

Much of the criticism has come from within the ranks of the middle class itself. The Urban League's Clarence Coleman sees the middle class as the buffer between the militants, whose aspirations are frequently unrealistic in terms of present possibilities, and the power elite which seems concerned to protect itself and its privileged positions from too rapid social change.

James A. Tillman, Jr., executive director of the Greater Minneapolis Fair Housing Program and a frequent writer on problems of social change, describes the Negro middle class as "that class of Negroes who have bought the inane, invalid, and self-defeating notion that the black man can be integrated into a hostile white society without conflict."

Tillman denounces the power elite as "the fixers and go-betweens who cover up rather than expose the violent nature of racism. They are," he declares, "the most dangerous clique in America."

Tillman's sentiments are echoed by Cecil Moore, militant civil rights attorney and head of the Philadelphia NAACP.

Moore, who himself came from an accomplished West Virginia family, insists that "the Negro middle class, and all those who consider themselves above the middle class, 'subsist on the blood of the brother down under,' the brother they are supposed to be leading. Who do these Negroes think they're kidding?" he asks, and then answers his own question. "They're kidding nobody but the white folks who are willing to pay 'philanthropy' to keep from having to come to grips with the central problem, which is 'full and complete citizenship for all Americans, *right now!*' "

Despite all such criticism, however, the Negro middle class has borne the brunt of the civil rights protest. Critics of the so-called "Black Bourgeoisie" have not always given them credit for the maturity and social responsibility upon which the Negro's fight for first-class citizenship has finally depended. The civil rights fight, at least insofar as it visualizes an integrated society, is a middle-class fight. The NAACP, CORE, the Urban League, and the followers of Dr. Martin Luther King are all middle-class. (Indeed, the lower-class Negro has yet to be stirred by the promise of integration. He is more concerned with such immediate needs as jobs and housing than with abstract values like integration. He looks neither to Martin Luther King nor to Roy Wilkins; in fact, the leader of the black masses has yet to appear.)

In Atlanta and other Southern cities during the massive sit-ins of 1962–63, housewives baked pies, made sandwiches, and provided transportation for the students. Negro businessmen donated food, gasoline, and other supplies. Then doctors, nurses, professors, and businessmen walked the picket lines. Similar middle-class support has assisted the activities of CORE in New York, Cleveland, and other cities in the North. Voter registration is essentially a middle-class project.

Middle-class leadership and support of the civil rights movement has not been without ambivalence. Desegregated schools frequently mean that Negro teachers will lose their jobs. Negro businessmen often lose their most competent clerical help to recently desegregated industries. Negro restaurants, drugstores, real estate firms, and the like may be adversely affected by desegregation. Some Negro churches have lost members to white churches. In a fully integrated society the Negro middle class would lose its identity. Indeed, it would cease to exist.

Some Negroes recognize all this, of course, and fight against it. Nor can it be said that the majority of the middle class is active in the rights struggle. What can be said is that the struggle is for the most part led, financed, and supported by the Negro middle class and, of course, its white allies.

Certainly Negro leadership has become a "profession," and in some cases a lucrative one. Yet most Negroes trying to help improve things are in search of neither fame nor fortune and may be themselves disadvantaged by the race issue. A. Maceo Walker and Jesse Turner of Memphis, for example, both executive officers of a sensitive banking business that has important white as well as Negro depositors, come to mind. These men and others like them have little to gain for themselves personally, yet they have given leadership to the civil rights movement in their city for years. Other cases could be cited across the country.

In Washington, I talked with the distinguished Negro attorney, Belford Lawson, and his wife, Marjorie McKenzie, who, as associate judge of the Juvenile Court there, is no less distinguished. The Lawsons were undisturbed about the "black backlash" against the Negro middle class, although they felt that the middle class was just beginning to realize its responsibilities to the Negro masses. Nor did they recognize a middle-class backlash against the lower class (which has been roundly criticized by some Negroes for rioting in the streets and undoing the patient and painful accomplishments of middle-class leaders).

"We must press on to the next phase," Lawson said. "And it would be foolish to wait until all of us have reached the place a few of us have reached today. Negroes, like other people, move at different rates of speed. Our circumstances vary. Now we have a handful of civil rights and no money. Our next front is economic. We want to buy stocks in banks and corporations and sit on their boards. Every time a Negro reaches an executive position in a major corporation, he is in a better position to help that Negro in the streets without a job."

Mr. Lawson believes that it is time to move on into the American mainstream. "Breaking into the white man's economy" he believes to be essential to any further progress on the part of Negroes. "In Washington," he says, "where many social and cultural affairs are integrated, many doors would open if the Negro would only push on them."

Negroes are pushing—for status and respectability and economic security. They are less concerned with integration for integration's sake than they are with being comfortable—middle-class—and unhindered in enjoying all that America has to offer. The riots in the city streets are not the work of sinister Communist agents, except where such agents move in to exploit an already festering social situation. Nor are they the work of hopheads and hoodlums bent on the destruction of the fruits of years of patient interracial effort.

They are the social expressions of pent-up anxiety and frustration which derive from the hopelessness of the conditions under which those people live. *They* cannot appropriate the "middle-class image," the American norm for democratic living.

I sat recently in a comfortable middle-class home in northwest Washington talking with Jerry Coward and his wife, both schoolteachers in the District of Columbia school system. "You know, when we moved into this neighborhood five years ago," Jerry said, "the whites all threatened to move out. A few stayed. And since that time two brand-new white families have moved in, right down the block. Professional people, too. When white people start moving into, instead of away from, a Negro neighborhood, I guess we've got it made."

I guess they have.

THE MEANING OF MALCOLM X*

The assassination of Malcolm X upset a good part of the American public. We were upset, and we tend to remain a bit on edge, *not* because Malcolm was a martyr to the cause of civil rights or because of any inherent contributions he may have made to the solution of our race problems, but because he was the symbol of violence and the spokesman for the violent "black man" in America. We remain uneasy because the murder of Malcolm X may well set off a Chinese-type "tong war" within the black nationalist factions striving for leadership of the masses in the Harlems of America.

We were aghast and dismayed by last summer's riots, by the looting and the wanton destruction of property, but at that time we were fortunate in at least two respects: the riots were not organized and led by any recognized leader, and they were riots against property rather than against people. True, they expressed the resentment and the hatred of the frustrated, penned-up Harlem lower class; but there were few instances of attacks against the human objects of this fury, which included the disinterested Negro middle class no less than the hated Jew and the "blue-eyed devils" whose commercial pres-

* Published in *The Christian Century*, April 7, 1965.

ence in Harlem is exasperatingly ubiquitous and universally resented.

RETURN TO WARY EXPECTANCY

For several months there had been an uneasy calm hanging over the dirty tenements and gaudy storefronts of Harlem. The return of Malclom X from his Afro-Asian junket was eyed with genuine apprehension by popular Negro leadership and with jubilant expectation by the black nationalist fringe. Malcolm was as cagey as always. Some Negro leaders thought they saw signs of a "constructive change" in his attitude toward racial goals and the proper techniques for attaining them. The more impatient activists were equally certain that Malcolm had brought them a kind of black-lettered message from García, and they were waiting for the word to be given.

Malcolm X himself was having other problems. He had left the country in disgrace and disharmony with the one black nationalist organization with a significant following, and on returning to Harlem he found himself in direct competition with the Black Muslims for leadership of the black dissidents for whom integration and assimilation are not viable solutions. His first order of interest was to stay alive, an interest neither he nor his followers nor the New York police proved adequate to protect.

The leadership of the Harlem masses is, at least in potential, an office of extraordinary power. It is also a hazardous undertaking. Thus far, with the possible exception of Marcus Garvey, no one has successfully mobilized the masses of America's most populous (and most shameful) black ghetto. Various self-styled leaders, usually oriented toward black nationalism or some other chauvinistic negritude, have had varying degrees of success in isolating a following, invariably small when measured against the numbers of potential converts who live in that steaming ghetto.

For the past decade or so the Black Muslims have had the largest and by far the best-organized following among the black nationalist groups in Harlem. For most of that period Malcolm himself had been their de facto leader, although policy was set by Elijah Muhammad in Chicago. So it was that Malcolm's defection from the Muslims and his subsequent return to Harlem as head of his Organization for Afro-American Unity brought him into direct conflict with the Black Muslim organization.

Negro leaders kept a wary eye on Malcolm precisely because they anticipated what did in fact occur, a black nationalist "tong war" which threatened the peace of the whole Harlem community and, indirectly, the leadership control responsible Negro leadership claimed to have. The exposure of the pro-Sino-Cuban Revolutionary Action movement caught most Americans of both races off guard because we are not accustomed to thinking in terms of Negro subversion. The myth of the satisfied Negro has spawned the myth of absolute loyalty. Both are fictions. While the overwhelming majority of the Negro population is loyal to the American flag and the American way of life, so is the overwhelming white majority. There are exceptions in both cases; the number of exceptions is related to the population ratio, the frequency of opportunity, and the quality of incentive, not to race.

Until just yesterday there were no nonwhite world powers of significance. And, more important, Negroes and their cause stood to gain nothing whatever by playing footsie with another *white* power. Times have changed; while we are shedding our negative stereotypes about the Negro we may as well be disabused of some other stereotypes as well.

The death of Malcolm X left Elijah Muhammad in temporarily unchallenged control of the largest black nationalist organization in the country. Nobody knows how many Black Muslims there are. Some defected to Malcolm X when he left the movement more than a year ago; others simply defected because Malcolm's ouster seemed to provide a good opportunity to get out and return to what ex-Muslim Aubrey Barnette calls "the outside world of reality."

INTEGRATION OR REVOLUTION?

It is a moot question whether Malcolm made any contributions to the Negro's struggle for freedom, whether he was a "catalyst to the cause" or just a loud and strident voice crying in some personal wilderness foreign to the real needs and aspirations of the nation's Negroes. It is even a silly question, for it presupposes a consensus among Negroes as to where they want to go and by what means they want to get there. Such a consensus of course does not exist—any more than does an American consensus of our role in (or out of) Vietnam.

Consensus obtains on the proper goals (but not on the proper methodology) among America's "responsible" *middle-class* leaders, and collectively they do represent the organized thrust of the American Negro's determination to be free. But we may not safely ignore the dissident masses merely because they are less articulate or more violent in their articulation, or because they are fragmented into many small groups of undetermined membership. There is a consensus among these groups, too, and it is not the consensus of the responsible middle class. To the various black nationalist fronts in Harlem and elsewhere Malcolm X was a potential "liberator," a man on a black horse who would someday lead them in a revolutionary struggle against the hated blue-eyed devils.

It does not promote the cause of responsible leadership to deny the importance of Malcolm X to the particular segment of people whose political and/or ideological leader he was, or sought to be; to do so is to deny by implication the threat he represented to the tranquillity and effectiveness of the more sophisticated procedures advanced by more acceptable leaders. Milton Galamison, for example, exists *and* has a following, however annoying that fact may be to more orthodox leadership; the Revolutionary Action movement is a fact, despite its embarrassing and treasonable implications. Similarly, Malcolm X made an impact on the minds of the black masses irrespective of his criminal past or his chauvinistic ideology. Had his turbulent life not been cut short, the chances are that his impact would have widened.

There are many Negroes who are not impressed by Christian philosophies of nonviolence because Christianity itself has so frequently been violent and because the yoke of oppression was for so long sanctioned by the church. Tens of thousands of others simply have not reached the level of sophistication which would enable them to understand the value and the dignity of nonviolent resistance. Indeed, relatively few Americans, whatever their race, are ideologically or psychologically prepared to suffer with the James Farmers and the Martin Luther Kings of today's black revolution. Certainly the men with the crash helmets and the cattle prods do not know or do not care what nonviolence is all about. So long as men like these are the accepted guardians of the status quo, Malcolm X and the Malcolm X's waiting to be discovered will have meaning for the black masses who live in the black ghettos of America.

DEMAGOGUE OR MARTYR?

As soon as Malcolm was dead his critics turned on him with the fervor of self-righteousness and his defenders sought to elevate him to sainthood and martyrdom. On the one hand, it was pointedly suggested that as a demagogue and a spokesman for violence Malcolm somehow deserved what he got at the Audubon ballroom that Sunday, the day before Washington's Birthday. He had been a thug, an addict, and a thief, it was argued; he was an ex-convict; he had made no contributions whatever to society.

There is a *non sequitur* here which honesty compels us to examine. It is contrary to the "American ideal" and Christian morality to hold a man's past against him if it can be shown that he has overcome that past. Man *is* redeemable; if he is not, surely preaching is in vain. Malcolm X rose above the errors of his youth. Whether or not one agrees with his solution to the race problem, it must be admitted that during the years he presumed himself a race leader he was, under the constant scrutiny of a hostile public, far more circumspect than many of our more "respectable" leaders and politicians. If anything, his past seemed to give him a unique insight into the nature of the problems with which he sought to deal. We owe it to him and to ourselves to acknowledge the facts.

On the other hand, those who saw in the returned pilgrim to Mecca a "new" Malcolm X were at best probably premature in their judgments. The underlying cause of the breach between Malcolm X and Elijah Muhammad was not so much a contest of power within the movement as a conflict of ideology. Malcolm X was a true revolutionary. It is not inconceivable that, given the time, the means, and the opportunity, Malcolm X would have committed an act of violence.

He was indoctrinated to believe that racial strife is the inevitable means of bringing about a reversal of the black man's status, and he passionately believed in and longed for that reversal. True, his conversion to Islam and his desire to be acceptable to orthodoxy may have ameliorated his aggressive tendencies; but the evidence that at the time of his death he was prepared to join the nonviolent crusade is scanty, if indeed it exists at all.

Malcolm X must be taken for what he was. He was a remarkably gifted and charismatic leader whose hatreds and resentments symbolized the dreadful stamp of the black ghetto, but a man whose philosophies of racial determination and whose commitments to violence made him unacceptable as a serious participant in peaceful social change. He had ideological followers—far more than the handful of men and women who belonged to the Organization of Afro-American Unity. His spirit will rise again, phoenix-like—not so much because he is worthy to be remembered as because the perpetuation of the ghetto which spawned him will not let us forget.

THE BRITISH SAY
THEY AREN'T PREJUDICED*

LONDON. "They're not like you, sir. You're an American. It's not that they're black, so much—they can't help that, I suppose. But if you'll pardon me, sir, they're filthy dirty. Most of them have tuberculosis. They spit in the street and they have venereal disease. Up in Birmingham and some other places, why, they're taking over the country."

The speaker was a very proper London taxi driver. He was talking about Britain's "dark million," the growing nonwhite population coming from the Commonwealth countries of Asia, Africa, and the Caribbean.

When my taxi pulled up in front of the American Embassy in Grosvenor Square, he said with an air of triumph as he opened the cab door: "You see, sir, I told you. You're an American. I could tell right off. The American colored are different from the nignogs we get here from the West Indies."

I tipped him and turned to go, but he called out after me: "God bless you, sir. I hope everything will turn out well for your people. And God bless your Dr. Martin Luther King! He is a great man!"

That very day in Selma, Alabama, American Negroes were still stunned from a savage attack made on them by Sheriff

* Published in *The New York Times Magazine*, November 14, 1965.

Jim Clark's forces the day before. But in Britain, I mused rue-fully, we are "different—and God bless Martin Luther King!"

A few days later I had lunch with a young M.P. at the House of Commons. "How do you assess the color problem in Britain?" I asked him.

"Well, first of all," he assured me, "it isn't at all like the racial problem in America. The British people, as you no doubt know, have absolutely no history of racialism. Our problem is primarily a physical problem—a problem of space and housing—particularly of housing. Many of our own people have been waiting years for housing. It's a matter of housing and jobs and trying to physically absorb a million immigrants into a situation that is already overcrowded."

Six months later the same M.P. was reluctant to discuss the problem at all. In the interim the Labor Government had pub-lished a white paper on the subject and clamped down on the number of Commonwealth immigrants to be allowed into the country. Three years earlier the Labor party had strongly opposed the then Conservative Government's restrictive legis-lation but had found its stand electorally embarrassing. Some Labor politicians are afraid that an even mildly liberal policy on immigration will cost them five or ten or even more seats at the next election.

Again and again throughout my visits in Britain I was to hear variations on the same theme: "We aren't prejudiced. We just don't have the facilities." Even the "coloreds" with whom I talked were reluctant to identify their problems with those of the Negro in America. "Our problems are different from yours," one young Jamaican professional told me.

What are the problems that are so "different"? The funda-mental problem is that Britain, for the first time in modern history (there were some Africans with the Roman legions in the Roman occupation of nearly two thousand years ago), has an influx of nonwhites in sufficiently large numbers to become conspicuous in London, Birmingham, Manchester, Bradford, Sheffield, and a half-dozen other cities and towns. As a result racial incidents have multiplied—and keep multiplying. While the frustrated Negroes in the Los Angeles ghettos were rampaging in an orgy of burning and pillaging, crosses were being burned in front of "immigrant" homes in Britain. Further, a chapter of the night-riding Ku Klux Klan has allegedly been exported to these racially divided islands. "Coloreds" have been beaten and threatened. For all its "differences," the problem, or at any rate the way the problem is expressed, seems familiar. In at least one instance, in the Midlands industrial city of Wolverhampton, a white mob armed with sticks and bottles laid siege to a colored residence in support of a white family involved in a trivial dispute over a footpath.

The enormity of the Los Angeles riots had a sobering effect on the British. Both the press and the people generally were noticeably restrained in their comments on the racial crisis in California. Perhaps they saw in the carnage of Los Angeles an example of what could happen in Birmingham, Manchester, or even London.

The "duskies" or "coloreds" so far constitute only 2 per cent of the population. Yet their presence has inspired troubles —political, psychological, and economic—far out of proportion to their numbers, and this in a country with a long history of racial tolerance. For a hundred years and more, Hindus, Africans, Malays, Chinese, West Indians, and countless other breeds have given dash to the majestic drabness of British officialdom, and their sons have been educated in the best British schools. In seaports such as Cardiff, Liverpool, and Southampton, Negro sailors and their families have lived for generations.

After the last war the United Kingdom opened its gates to the people of every Commonwealth nation, recognizing them as citizens of Britain and allowing them to vote after a residence of six months. It was the nonwhite countries that stood to benefit most—India and Pakistan with their teeming millions of unemployed and steadily rising birth rates, the crowded West Indies with a sick economy.

As early as 1952 Britain was already in trouble because of her policy of open immigration. Leaders from some of the towns where immigration was heaviest appealed to the government for help in assimilating the colored migrants. The Colonial Office took the position that it could assume no responsibility for the migrants as they were British citizens who, just as any other citizens, were the responsibility of their local governments. Not until race riots (minor by American standards) occurred in Nottingham and in London's Notting Hill and Paddington in 1958 were the British shocked into an awareness of the increasing complexity of the race problem.

At that time there were only 200,000 coloreds in the country. Now there are well over a million, including an estimated 535,000 Pakistanis and Indians (and a few thousand Chinese and Africans) and 660,000 West Indians. Birmingham alone has a colored population of more than 70,000 (in a total population of 1,115,000). In some of the smaller cities the nonwhite population is 30 to 40 per cent of the total.

In an effort to control this rising tide, restrictions on immigration were established by the Conservative Government under the Commonwealth Immigrants Act of 1962. Control is exercised by a system of "employment vouchers" originally issued in three categories: "A," for applicants with jobs waiting in Britain; "B," for applicants skilled in a trade or profession short of workers; and "C," for veterans who have served the British Government in war and for all others who do not fall into the first two categories.

Physicians from India, nurses from the West Indies, and a few other skilled persons have no problems in getting "A" vouchers. Further, the transport and hospital services are particularly dependent upon low-paid colored labor, admitted on "A" or "B" vouchers, to fill jobs as drivers, conductors, orderlies, nurses' aides, and interns. While the labor unions are hostile toward nonwhites, for the most part, there is no objection to their working the late mill shifts that white workers do not want, or doing menial labor such as street-cleaning.

Last year some 20,000 Commonwealth citizens were permitted to come to Britain to work and were accompanied or joined by 50,000 dependents. However, this was only part of the story. The 1962 Commonwealth Immigrants Act has many loopholes; thousands of other coloreds—particularly Pakistanis—entered illegally. Traffic in forged vouchers and other such devices is brisk, and there appeared to be no way to close all the gaps. The problem reached the stage, in fact, where high-level consultations were held with Commonwealth governments.

Then last August, Herbert Bowden, leader of the House of Commons, announced that while Britain recognized "the valuable contribution" of Commonwealth immigrants, "nearly everyone appreciates that there is a limit to the number of immigrants that this small and overcrowded country can absorb." Therefore, he said, the Labor Government would reduce the number of permits from 20,000 a year to 8,500 and eliminate provisions for admitting immigrants in category "C" of the voucher system. Thus Labor—which had fought immigration controls when the Conservatives opposed them—in effect joined the Opposition. Furthermore, a public-opinion poll indicated that the government's "get tough" policy had the approval of three of four voters, and that more than 50 per cent of the voters thought that restrictions against colored immigration should be even more severe.

Although many Britons wish the coloreds would quietly go back to where they came from, the coloreds have come to stay. (But not all of them: the Pakistanis and the Indians frequently stay only long enough to buy land at home and then return there.)

It is the West Indians who generally plan to remain. Many of them consider themselves "black Englishmen," and they do not conceive it strange that they should want to live in London. They work to buy houses and then send for their families. A house is not only a status symbol; in an economy where housing is tight it can also be the way to wealth.

Housing is hard to come by. In the London community of Brixton I talked with a Jamaican who had just bought a house. He had saved for four years, and then he had borrowed all he could get from his friends. He said that the agent had substantially overcharged him, but that he knew he was paying a color tax and accepted it, since he could do nothing about it. What he did not know was that the house had a white "sitting tenant" who insisted on his right to continue occupying his apartment at the same rent.

The new landlord was beside himself with rage and fear. Every room in his house would have to bring in a certain income if he was to meet the inflated notes he was obligated to pay. The white tenant could find nowhere to go at the rent he was paying. Everybody was unhappy (except possibly the real estate agent, who had made a killing).

Many coloreds who have been stuck with white sitting tenants have resorted to "Rachmanism," a kind of harassment practiced by Peter Rachman, the late and infamous white slum landlord. His techniques ranged all the way from playing the radio full blast after midnight to encouraging the committing of indecencies in tenement halls and doorways. The whites (already primed to believe that the coloreds were filthy) would move out and their rooms be let quickly to coloreds willing to pay inflated rents. Colored landlords who have adopted these techniques defend themselves by arguing that if they could buy at true market prices there would be no urgency to dispossess "sitting" whites.

Another source of friction is lower-class white resentment of the thrift and industry shown by the colored newcomers. The Asians are condemned for "sending money out of the country without paying taxes on it," and for working double shifts and upsetting the labor market. The West Indians are resented for buying houses (even at inflated prices) when native whites still need housing, and for buying flashy cars on the installment plan when all the whites in the neighborhood are walking.

A hostile Briton is inclined to make no distinction among nonwhite immigrants. (One civil servant referred to them all as "niggers" and said he'd "just as soon throw in the Maltese, the Cypriotes and the Greeks as well.") "Coloreds" and "immigrants" are the polite terms. At other times they are referred to as "wogs," "nignogs," "wallah-wallahs," "coolies," "blacks," and "darkies."

Some white Britons do have orders of preference—or at least orders of denigration—where nonwhites are concerned. Some prefer the Indians, others the Africans. Generally, it seems that West Indians are both more readily accepted ("They're like us except they're black") and more readily rejected ("They're nothing but savages"). The West Indians speak English and are thoroughly grounded in English values. They play cricket and become homeowners, and they are intensely loyal to the British Crown and to the British way of life insofar as they understand it and are permitted to become a part of it.

The Pakistanis, on the other hand, keep to themselves, refuse to learn the language, and have dietary and religious practices strange to Britons. Therefore legends about their personal habits quickly gain currency. They have been accused of bringing in tuberculosis, and while they may not have the disease when they arrive, the incidence among Pakistanis living in Britain is many times that of the national average. Health authorities attribute the high rate to an unaccustomed climate, improper diet, and generally poor living conditions. In an effort to save money and because housing is hard to find, as many as twenty to thirty male Pakistanis may live together in one house, using the beds in shifts.

The immigrants, particularly the West Indians, are also held responsible for a high rate of venereal disease. This may be true; many are far from their families and, being excluded from respectable social contacts, turn to prostitutes for feminine companionship. It is hard to tell whether the immigrants are resented more for their venereal diseases or for their association with white prostitutes.

You can recognize a West Indian community by the gay, tropical blue, red, and yellow paint on the façades of the old Victorian houses. No less picturesque are the West Indians themselves. They come off the planes or down the gangplanks in brilliant silk skirts of greens and reds and impossible straw hats set at jaunty angles. On Saturday nights they have "commercial" house parties (known as "house rent" parties among Negroes in America) and with their guitars and steel drums soon set the neighborhood athrob with Caribbean rhythms.

Their white neighbors (who don't go to the parties) say they are wild and rowdy. The policemen who do go (at the request of the neighbors) say the coloreds are no noisier than the Irish. And when it comes to criminal activity, fewer colored immigrants are involved, in proportion, than whites.

Prejudice against coloreds in public facilities has led the Labor Government to introduce a race-relations bill reminiscent of the 1964 Civil Rights Act in the United States. It would outlaw discrimination "on grounds of color, race, or ethnic or national origins" in hotels, restaurants, pubs, theaters, and public housing. However, it is conspicuously silent on employment and private housing.

Segregation in the schools has never been tolerated. The Ministry of Education recently directed a circular to local authorities recommending that the proportion of immigrants in any school or class be held to a third of the total, lest "serious strains arise." And in an effort to reassure English parents concerned by the great influx of immigrants, Anthony Crosland, the Minister of Education, said: "We want to maintain standards for English children as well as coping with the special problem of the immigrant children."

While Britain's colored leaders welcome the government's recognition of the color problem, they feel that the proposed anti-discrimination legislation does not go far enough. Some are convinced that the colored immigrant's salvation is in his own hands and depends on his own enterprise, such as a new savings bank that opened recently to provide immigrant mortgages. The consensus is that the British immigrants could learn a lot from American Negro business and financial leaders who have had to organize their own institutions in order to become independent of prejudiced whites.

A new organization called the Campaign Against Racial Discrimination—CARD—grew out of a conference with the Rev. Dr. Martin Luther King last December. It is headed by David Pitt, a physician from Trinidad, and Mrs. Selma James, Jewish wife of C. L. R. James, a long-time Trinidad Socialist and political writer.

Mrs. James explained that CARD was committed to "coordinating the work of existing organizations and acting as a clearing house for information about the fight against discrimination in Britain." She emphasized that it was not an affiliate of Dr. King's Southern Christian Leadership Conference and was not committed to any philosophies "other than its own." More than twenty-five immigrant organizations representing

Africans, West Indians, Pakistanis, Indians, and English sympathizers are already affiliated with CARD.

A more militant organization is the Racial Adjustment Action Society led by Michael De Freitas, a West Indian Negro who was a close friend and admirer of the late Malcolm X. Like Malcolm, Michael (also known as Michael X) is a Muslim and unstinting in his denunciation of the ruling whites. His movement is said to have a membership of around 50,000 and to be growing fast.

Under the influence of R.A.A.S., 500 West Indian, Indian, and Pakistani spinners joined in a sit-down strike at a mill in Preston, Lancashire, last May. Many political eyebrows were raised at this unprecedented show of color solidarity among these three diverse racial and religious groups. It could be a sign of the times.

It would appear that the battle has been joined in Britain and that, like the United States, she has come full circle from studied ignorance of a problem, to intelligent awareness, and finally to confrontation and action. Make no mistake about it. White Britain's most desperate fear is that the "dark million" will grow to *two* "dark millions." And then perhaps to *three!* Who can say? But that is not the issue. The issue there, as here, is whether the Anglo-Saxon with all his social and political sophistication can learn to live comfortably with diversity.

A British columnist complains: "Many want to keep Britain white, not because they hate other races, but because they love Britain; not because they despise the stranger from distant lands, but because they cherish the familiar in their own." What a strange sound to come from old John Bull, who for four hundred years of conquest never seemed to have thought much about it.

THE ABSENT FATHER HAUNTS
THE NEGRO FAMILY*

Under pressure of law, public opinion, and Negro militancy, progress in civil rights has reached the point where many Americans assume that the practical end of discrimination is only a matter of time. But even the end of formal discrimination falls short of the distant goal: full integration of the Negro into American life. Nor can true integration be achieved until the nation—and the Negro—solves a crucial and immediate problem: how to "Americanize" the fragile, fractured Negro family.

The Negro in America was never a "black Anglo-Saxon," though sometimes he tried to be. He was never simply "another ethnic group" to be assimilated into the mainstream. His family structure is unique in American society.

The U.S. family is primarily patriarchal. The husband and father is the chief breadwinner, carrying the responsibility for his wife and children. Even in families where husband and wife supposedly share equally in making decisions, our society regards the male as "more equal." The law defines this relationship; custom supports and rewards it. But the majority of Negro families do not follow the U. S. custom and are appropriately penalized. Because women have assumed pri-

* Published in *The New York Times Magazine*, November 28, 1965.

mary responsibility as head of the family, the matriarchal Negro household is at a distinct disadvantage in competing for its rightful share of benefits offered by American society.

About 25 per cent of Negro families are headed by women who have no husbands. These are families where the male is absent because of divorce, separation, or desertion, and do not include families with illegitimate children which have never included a male parent.

The easy explanation of the shattered Negro family puts the blame on the Negro male, caricatured as shiftless and lazy. A more socially acceptable reason attributes the matriarchal family structure to super-aggressive females. In fact, the blame rests on the horrors of a slave society which stripped the Negro male of his masculinity and condemned him to a eunuch-like existence in a culture which venerates masculine primacy.

There are no discontinuities in history. Negroes today (like any other people) are largely the product of yesterday. And American slavery, the "yesterday" of the American Negro, ended only a hundred years ago. For 250 years before emancipation, slavery ordered the lives, the thinking, and the behavior of white people in one way and of Negroes in quite another.

American slavery was a different institution from contemporary slavery in South America, Portugal, Africa, or from ancient slavery in Greece and Rome. It developed its own institutionalized values uniquely designed to promote its own ends. Its peculiar impingement upon the Negro in America inescapably conditioned his values, his behavior, and his future.

When Negroes were slaves, neither the law nor the slave owners recognized marriage between slaves. Males of prime physical condition were mated with females, like so many cattle. Children were left with the mother, giving the Negro mother an early, exclusive interest in the family and forcing upon her full responsibility for its care. In those instances where a male and female were permitted to live together longer than necessary for procreation, the Negro father (he could hardly be called a husband) had absolutely no control over his family or its fortunes. Children were seized and sold. Often the father himself was sold away from his family, never to see them again.

The psychology of castration was viciously applied in other ways too. No Negro man was given a title of respect, a practice which continues in much of the rural South today. A Negro man was simply "Sam," "Jim," or frequently "boy," no matter what his age. He was never "Mister." If he was living with a woman—the nearest thing to marriage—he was known as "Hattie's Sam" or "Mandy's Jim," again denying him a position as head of the family. And if the white man wanted Hattie or Mandy for himself, the Negro male had to step aside; interference as a "husband" meant severe punishment and, not infrequently, death.

When the Negro was freed from bondage all the laws Congress could muster were not effective in wholly transferring him from the category of slave to the category of citizen.

The slaves were freed without any provision for their economic or social well-being. They were almost totally uneducated, for to have educated a slave was a criminal offense. They had no money and no homes. And they were concentrated in a politically and economically distressed society hostile to their presence as freedmen. Even those who made their way to the North quickly found themselves unwelcome, for as indigents with low skills they threatened to glut the unskilled labor market and become a burden on the tax-paying citizenry.

Because of her peculiar relationship to the white woman as a servant, and because she was frequently the white man's mistress, the Negro woman occasionally flouted the rules of segregation. Her immunity was by no means absolute, but because she often reigned supreme in the white man's kitchen and nursery she could, in times of crisis, "talk to the man" and get concessions that made life a little more bearable for herself and her children.

The practice of sending the Negro woman to do business with the white man became quickly established in the Negro-white pattern of relations. In the ruptured economy of the postwar South, Negro women were frequently paid more than their menfolk and they could ordinarily find jobs in domestic service while their men walked the streets looking for work.

"Freedom" did not improve the image of the Negro male or give him a sense of security as head of the family. He remained a semi-slave, and his slavery was rooted in the centuries he had spent in America.

If you want to understand his hatreds, his resentments, his castration as a husband and father, look back a hundred years. And if you ask why in one hundred years he has not overcome the past, it is because the past has never died: every day, every hour of that hundred years of semi-freedom has had to be rewon day by day from the prejudice which still promotes, openly or covertly, the old ways of slavery. The Negro did not earn rewards for being manly, courageous, or assertive, but for being accommodating—for fulfilling the stereotype of what he has been forced to be.

We may note, in the interest of keeping perspective, that some stable Negro families with male heads existed before and after slavery. Before the Civil War some free Negroes in the South and North maintained family structures and customs as closely analogous to those in the prevailing white culture as circumstances would permit. A few upper-class Negro families, mostly along the Atlantic Coast, have an unbroken tradition of more than a hundred years of social stability and cultural progress. And in the Deep South a handful of Negro families that date to slavery, or the first decades after emanci-

pation, testify to the Negro's determined attempt to overcome the scars of thralldom.

The symptoms of the Negro family's enduring sickness are
everywhere evident today.

The Negro crime rate is higher by far than the national
average. The rate of illegitimacy is higher—regardless of the
inconsistency of reporting procedures—and may be as high as
25 per cent. Negro drug addiction, especially among juveniles,
is much higher than among whites—dramatic evidence of the
attempt to escape the rigors of living in a society which for
them bears little promise for a better future. The percentage
of Negro high-school dropouts, again far above the national
average, reflects the same sense of Negro hopelessness.

This is social sickness of epidemic proportions, and it
spreads with the steady deterioration of the Negro family.

As the basic unit of socialization for the young, the family
needs the presence of both parents if children are to learn the
values and expectations of society. But socialization is a continuing experience which affects not only children but parents
as well. A "family man" is much less likely to lapse into criminal activity than one without ties and responsibilities.

The absent father has not been, until recently, a particularly disturbing factor among Negroes themselves (except for
educated Negroes who were particularly sensitive to the white
man's blanket charge of racial immorality). Any male in the
average Negro family might function as a father-figure:
uncles, older brothers, grandfather, even cousins. Similarly a
grandmother or aunt was frequently "mama" to a brood of
children not biologically her own.

Television has been one factor in sensitizing the Negro
child to the fact that his family is different. Another increasingly important factor is the integrated school. In their association with white children from complete families, Negro
kids learn early that something is different about their own

households. This awareness is sharpened even further by white teachers who have Negro pupils for the first time. As a Negro teacher in a newly integrated school explained it: "My white colleagues get *so* frustrated when they ask little brown Johnny, 'What does your father do?' and Johnny says he doesn't know. Then they ask, 'Well, Johnny, what does your father look like? Is he big and tall?' and Johnny says he doesn't know. And finally they say, 'Well, all right, Johnny, what is your father's name?' and Johnny says he doesn't know."

The divorce rate among Negro families is 5.1 per cent, compared to 3.8 per cent among whites. But divorces are expensive, and the rate of desertion—the poor man's divorce—is even higher. In many cases the psychological strain of being a member of a family he cannot support because of unemployment or lack of skills is too much for the Negro husband, and he simply disappears. More often he "deserts" so that his family may become eligible for relief payments, since the family is often better off on relief than depending on the uncertainties of a job. In any event, only a minority of Negro children will complete high school in a two-parent home.

Among middle-class Negroes the battered male ego is frequently a factor in divorce or separation. The Negro professional is in actual or vicarious contact with the American mainstream. He knows his white counterpart is the chief breadwinner and head of the family in *his* home, and the Negro is acutely sensitive to the possibility of his own failings in these respects.

As tangible goods accumulate and increasingly important decisions are made, most Negro men become restive and uncomfortable if they are married to women who outearn them and who assume the prerogatives of family leadership as a corollary to their earning power. In Atlanta, for example, I asked a young Negro woman, a teacher, "Who is head of the family at your house?" She thought for a moment, then answered: "Well, Jack is now, but when I get my raise, I'll be head, because I'll be making twenty-seven dollars more than he will."

The problem is considerably more formidable than such naïveté, I assure you. The Negro female has had the responsibility of the Negro family for so many generations that she accepts it, or assumes it, as second nature. Many older women have forgotten why the responsibility devolved upon the Negro woman in the first place, or why it later became institutionalized. And young Negro women do not think it is absurd to reduce the relationship to a matter of money since many of them probably grew up in families where the only income was earned by their mothers: their fathers may not have been in evidence at all.

Even in middle-class Negro families where the husband earns more than his wife, the real cement holding the marriage may be status and "appearances" rather than a more fundamental attachment. The Negro wife who grew up in a matriarchal home finds it difficult to assent to male leadership in the family; the Negro husband with a similar family history may be overanxiously insistent on male prerogatives in order to align his family in what he conceives to be the American tradition.

I know a prominent professor in Atlanta who has taught there for fifteen years while his wife worked as a teacher in her hometown several hundred miles away. They see each other at Christmas and for a brief period at the end of his summer term. This respectable arrangement obviates, or at least postpones, the problem of who will be head of the family —at the price of maintaining a one-parent household.

The task of giving the Negro husband and father a status in keeping with the larger society requires a basic change in established patterns of Negro education, training, and employment.

More Negro women go to college than men, just the reverse of the white educational pattern. Six per cent of all female professionals are Negroes, while just a shadow over 1 per cent of all male professionals are Negroes. Negro females do better in school, too, probably reflecting the low incentive of the Negro male who frequently feels that even if he graduates, he still won't be getting anywhere.

The long tradition of educating the girls in the Negro families is rooted in the system of segregated employment which limited sharply the Negro male's prospects of finding a job commensurate with college training. In the typical Negro family the boys leave school and go to work early, frequently pooling their earnings for the education of their sisters. The process inevitably produces a pronounced imbalance in the ratio of educated women to educated men, reinforcing the disproportionate power and prestige of the Negro woman in the family.

Having to "marry down," if she marries at all, is a common experience of the Negro woman and one which perpetuates the matriarchal pattern while fostering dissatisfaction, desertion, and divorce. For that reason, certain Negro colleges are famous as hunting grounds for eligible men, and the tuition of many an indigent medical school student has been paid by the doting parents of aspiring daughters.

The ratio of Negro college men to women is changing slowly as employment opportunities for Negro men are broadened. In time the existing disparity as a distinctive feature of Negro life may disappear, but not until Negroes can try for success in fields closed to them for so long, and not until the incentives of Negro youth can be sharply increased.

The problem of education is, of course, interwoven with the question of jobs. Since 1930 the ratio of Negro unemployment to white employment has hovered steadily at about two to one.

The working husband of any race is usually the key to family stability; when the husband loses his job it represents the point at which the family may begin to deteriorate. His loss of self-esteem, the inability to support his family, dependence upon some social agency or the wife's earnings—all these factors generally presage more difficult problems to come. In the case of the Negro family, with its historic weaknesses and the tentative nature of male leadership, a prolonged period of unemployment can be disastrous. The family may break up completely and in the long run society has to pay.

The problem is far larger than the individual Negro family; it is bigger than the limited resources of the Negro lower class, which is most affected. The Johnson Administration, using the pioneering report on the Negro family by Daniel P. Moynihan as a point of departure, has recognized the dimensions of the crisis and inaugurated the most comprehensive series of social rehabilitation programs ever designed by the federal establishment.

Even that will not be enough. The government can make available better schools, better housing, and better opportunities for employment. It can enforce the laws protecting the franchise and the right to public accommodations. But the government cannot establish a pattern of family relationships which will foster the values needed to make all this meaningful and effective. Only the Negro can save his family. The substantive help of law and the government is essential, of course, but the incentive, the motivation which can transform the Negro predicament into a shining achievement of the Great Society, must come from within the group.

The white man destroyed the Negro family and kept it weak by preserving the psychology of slavery, thinly disguised as racial discrimination and prejudice. But the white man cannot give back the values he took away.

For years myopic but well-meaning whites have been challenging the Negro to pull himself up by his own bootstraps, even though the Negro didn't have either boots or straps. The white man was looking at his own boots and imagining the Negro owned a pair too. The "straps" of the Negro's family problem are not encouraging, but he must work with what he has.

THIRTY-FOUR MILLION POOR:
RIGHT HERE IN
AFFLUENT AMERICA

It was almost dark and we instinctively moved away from the shadows of the building as we approached the figure hunched against the wall outside the small, neighborhood bar. We were in the heart of the black ghetto of West Oakland, California. All day we had been hunting poverty, and we had found it. We found it in the shrill, staccato complaints of the Mexican-American women who met with the "government man" in their tiny basement kitchens with the dripping laundry hanging from the pipes overhead. We found it in the sullen, angry stares of Negroes, gathered on the street corners, or sitting in tight little knots on the stoops of the dilapidated tenements—Negroes who didn't want to be studied any more by white men from Washington (or by their Negro associates, either). But we found poverty at its worst in the eyes of the children —children who seemed to be everywhere. There was something wrong with their eyes. There was no light there. No sparkle. And even as they played in the gutters, kicking cans and throwing stones, one could not help being struck by the dull opacity which gave their eyes and their faces the haunting eeriness of despair and hopelessness.

The "government man" was Eugene Foley, (then) Under Secretary of Commerce, and he was in Oakland anonymously to appraise for himself the depth of the other half of the American dilemma—persistent poverty in the midst of affluence. On an impulse the government man headed directly toward the figure hunched against the tavern.

"Pardon me, sir, what kind of work do you do?"

The man pushed himself away from the wall and peered intently at each of us in turn. As he straightened out of the anonymity of his huddle in the shadows, we could see that he was a ruggedly built Negro, maybe fifty years old. Hard to tell. He could have been sixty—or forty.

"I do most any kind of work when I can get it," he said simply. Then with a note of cautious hopefulness in his voice, he asked, "Y'all gentlemen lookin' for somebody to do some work? Most likely I can do it." He tugged significantly at a pair of worn leather gloves in his hip pocket.

"We don't have any work for you to do just now," said Mr. Foley. "But I'm from Washington, and we're trying to find ways to help people like you."

The man leaned back against the wall.

"Washington ain't give folks like me no *real* jobs since WPA way back in Tennessee," he said. "There've been a whole lot of jobs, but *we* don't git 'em. We ain't supposed to. I ain't had a decent job in six years, going on seven. And I ain't worked three days running for six months. Man can't feed a family on that kind of work," he concluded bitterly. "Two days ago was the last time I worked. I made four dollars."

"How much of a family do you have?" I asked the man.

"Me, I got nine children and a sick wife. This time last week I had ten children. The littlest one died. The doctor said he didn't get the proper nourishment. But I done all I could. I done *everything* I could." He drew himself up and looked at Mr. Foley.

"Do y'all want to know how come I'm standing outside

this tavern? Well, I'm waiting for somebody in there to git drunk enough for me to roll him for a piece of change." His voice rose defiantly, almost hysterically, it seemed to me. "I've just naturally *got* to have a piece of money to buy my children some milk and bread. They're hungry! I ain't going home tonight with nothing in my hand!"

I gave the man a twenty-dollar bill and watched with satisfaction—*and guilt*—as he hurried into the grocery store across the street. When he emerged a few minutes later with both arms full of groceries, the Under Secretary of Commerce said, "I wish with all my heart that we in the government could be so simply and so instantaneously effective as you have been right now."

In Memphis I sat in the comfortable offices of the Wurzburg Bros. Paper Co. and talked with Richard Wurzburg, a bright young officer of the company, and a recent graduate of the University of Tennessee. Around the modern Wurzburg plant is a Negro slum, and although the area has—through the instrumentality of urban renewal—"Negro removal" some call it—largely been denuded of its once vast acreage of dilapidated wooden shacks, a few stark tenements and three-room row houses still stand in crazy and defiant isolation—waiting the inevitable day of the bulldozer and the wrecking ball. In these shacks and tenements are the poor—the Negro poor. They pick a little cotton in the fall. The big open trucks and aging, multicolored buses creak ominously through the littered streets long before daylight to round up their human cargo for the vast cotton plantations of the Mississippi delta and eastern Arkansas. At night—long after dark—the trucks and buses creak back again and deposit the drained and aching bodies under the occasional lampposts, from whence they disperse into the night clutching in knotted handkerchiefs and string-tied tobacco sacks the four, five, or six dollars that represent a "good" day's work.

By winter the money is all gone. The "coal man" walks slowly behind his truck through the hard and brittle streets beating his arms to keep warm and crying out his market song —which could be called quaint if it were not so ominous and true:

> Coal! Come git your Coal!
> Lawd, it's gonna be cold in the morning
> And you ain't gonna have no fire!

Lawd, it's cold *now!* But the thin wisps of blue smoke coming from the low chimneys of the shacks between the Wurzburg plant and the Booker T. Washington High School suggest the burning of newspapers and magazines rather than coal and wood.

I scan the streets and the driveways for the Cadillacs and the Oldsmobiles that are popularly supposed to mark the houses of the Negro poor. They are not there. There are *some* cars to be sure. But they are inevitably Fords and Chevys, many of them permanently parked on concrete blocks of Coke cases, with missing wheels, missing engines, missing tops, fenders, or bumpers.

I walked with Mr. Wurzburg to the loading dock of the plant and watched the children in the streets shivering against the cold as they paused from darting in and out among the traffic. This was not by any means the poorest neighborhood. To see the really poor, you have to go to North Memphis or further out south. The Wurzburg plant is on the perimeter of the city center, barely six or eight blocks from downtown. Although there are still some slum pockets even closer to the very heart of the business area, urban renewal and freeway construction have scraped most of the central city slums away.

Mr. Wurzburg was talking about the culture of the poor. "We hire a good bit of unskilled labor," he explained, "some

Negroes, but mostly whites. Most of the whites come in here to Memphis from eastern Arkansas, northern Mississippi, and southern Missouri. The blacks come from the Mississippi delta —right off the plantations."

"Maybe the stories of poor Negroes buying Cadillacs are exaggerated," he said. "But poor people, whatever their color, do sometimes do things that are hard for the rest of us to understand. On the whole, the poorest tend to be the least educated, and poorly educated people, black or white, don't buy our standards of value. Their absenteeism is higher. They are more likely to have severe domestic problems. And they get into debt and have their wages garnisheed over *frivolous* purchases, seldom over necessities. We have a colored worker who has all of his suits tailor-made, but we have to advance him money for his rent. But then we have a white worker whose wages are being garnisheed to pay for an elaborate electric guitar he can't play but keeps on display in his home as a sort of status symbol."

Who are these poor Americans who overspend, "lay off" from the job (if they have one), buy "status symbols," and have more children than they can feed?

First of all (a revealing fact to many Americans) is that poverty is indifferent to race, and that it exists in all sections of the country. It frequently assumes bizarre forms and produces behavior decidedly at variance with standard middle-class norms and values. On the other hand, the poor never cease to strive to be a part of that other America from which they are excluded by lack of opportunity. There are countless hundreds of Negro children on the backwoods plantations of Mississippi and Alabama who have never had a toy that was not "home made" out of bamboo, bucket tops, bits of baling wire, and the like, or who have never worn shoes, or who do not know anybody who went further than the fourth grade, yet who have a moral dignity and self-restraint we associate in our fantasies only with the "best people." There are poor whites in Appalachia who, while they may not own a change of clothing for every member of the family, insist that no proper household should be without a television set, *whether or not it works*, or a washing machine, even if it has to be filled with water toted from the nearest creek.

Where are the poor? They are in the South, the North, the East, the West, and the Central States. They are in the cities *and in the suburbs*, and on the farms. They are in the black ghettos of Harlem and the Chicago South Side. But they are "Uptown" on the Chicago North Side, too, where they come (bearing the purest Anglo-Saxon heritage) from the hill country of Kentucky, Virginia, and Tennessee. They are in the sparse settlements of the Upper Michigan Peninsula where $2,500 may be a pretty good year's wages. Three hundred thousand of them follow the crops as migrant workers. A disproportionate number of the poor are American Indians, on and off the reservations.

In terms of statistical aggregates, recent studies show that the South has most of the nation's poor with about four million families there earning less than $3,000 per year. Next highest concentration is in the north-central part of the country where two million families are below the poverty level. The Northeast has one and a half million poor families, and the West slightly over a million. Of these eight-plus million families—between thirty-five and forty million individual Americans—15 per cent live on farms; 25 per cent live in our central cities; and 60 per cent live in rural, non-farm areas and suburban districts.

In terms of absolute numbers, poor whites outnumber poor Negroes by a considerable degree, but the *percentage* of poor Negroes is much higher. A Negro family is two and a half times more likely to be poor than a white family and is much more likely to remain poor. In 1963, when the median income of white families was $6,548 per year, only 12 per cent of America's white families were below the poverty line. Statistics for the same year show that the median income for non-white families was only $3,465 per year, and 42 per cent of all nonwhite families were classified poor, this despite the fact that Appalachia, covering parts of eleven states involving relatively few Negroes, showed an incidence of poverty 50 per cent greater than the rest of the country.

In a further breakdown of the poverty mass, figures from the Social Security Administration show that 15.7 per cent of the white children under eighteen (in 1963) were poor, while 60 per cent of nonwhites in that age group were poor. Thirteen per cent of the whites eighteen or over were poor; but 40 per cent of the nonwhites above eighteen were poverty-stricken. Forty per cent of all families headed by women were below the poverty level, a fact which has grave implications for the Negro subculture which tends to be strongly matri-centric in the lower classes where poverty is a concomitant to the existence of every second family. Statistically speaking, today's American family has the best chance of being adequately provided for if the head of the family is male, white, and between the ages of twenty-five and sixty-four. Those who do not fit these requirements have to take their chances against the odds.

Can the odds be reduced? This is, of course, the crucial question. This is what the "Great Society's" celebrated "War on Poverty" is all about. In his first State of the Union message, President Lyndon B. Johnson committed himself and his office to the rescue of those "who live on the outskirts of hope —some because of their poverty, and some because of their color, and all too many because of both." To the swift relief of "that other nation within a nation—the poor whose distress has not captured the conscience of Americans," he pledged that: "This Administration today, here and now, declares un-conditional war on poverty in America."

The War on Poverty represents the grand ideal of an ideal-istic President who has himself walked close to many who have known the bitterness and hopelessness of want. To pur-sue the elusive will-o'-the-wisp he visualizes as the "good life" for all America, President Johnson chose Sargent Shriver, the able and energetic brother-in-law to the Brothers Kennedy, to head the Office of Economic Opportunity and to direct the war's wide-ranging programs of job training, relief, and reme-dial education; Head Start (preschool) programs for deprived children, Job Corps for high-school dropouts, Community Action Programs to encourage and help the poor regain con-fidence in themselves, clean up their own neighborhoods, and aspire for the values of the middle class. No one can say that the ideas are not well conceived. Their fulfillment could con-tribute immeasurably to the total welfare of the country and to the remaking of the American image as a nation which cares for its own.

The unfortunate truth is, however, that two and a half years and two and a half billion dollars later, the odds have not been significantly reduced, and the capture of the Amer-ican conscience seems not to have been accomplished. What *has* been accomplished is a tremendous proliferation of offices and programs (well-intentioned, no doubt) which have inter-posed yet another bureaucratic jungle between substantial help and the people who suffer the wrenching inconvenience of being poor in an affluent society.

There have been some skirmishes won in "The War," but as in so many other wars, there is public confusion among the brass about goals and objectives, strategy and timing. Jealousy about the prerogatives of leadership is intensified by the polit-ical appointment of too many general officers. There are also too many junior-grade officers of the idealistic sort getting in the way of the professionals—who are, for the most part, rather firmly mortized to yesterday's ideas. There is much duplication of effort. Overfunding, under-funding, delayed funding, and non-funding of various projects held at various times to be essential to the successful prosecu-tion of "The War" make for uncertain logistics and the failure to produce the instantaneous results the reluctant taxpayers want to see for their money. Worst of all, there is a deep sus-picion among some of the chief "warriors" about the people they have undertaken to liberate. They don't trust the poor. Some of them—and not a few of the taxpayers who, against their private will and better judgment, are forced to help un-derwrite "The War"—despise the poor for being poor. In their hearts the suspicion that being poor is the poor's own fault is rooted firmly in a religious tradition and watered daily by the mistaken belief that being poor means also being black.

In a society where the Horatio Alger myth is the justifica-tion of wealth and the Protestant ethic is the explanation of poverty, there is little wonder that the poor are so frequently looked upon, and treated, as being distinctively lesser beings. For with a little initiative, could they not (like so many other once poor Americans) "pull themselves up by their boot-straps"? Those who fail must therefore fail for lack of indus-triousness, a sure sign of other defects abhorrent to God and man.

That we are able to persist in the maintenance of such archaic attitudes in the face of some rather insistent realities can only be attributed to the profound social ignorance which characterizes a society which values money more than it does human dignity and human life. One of the first orders of the new Reagan regime in California was to move to close "in the interest of economy" the thirteen State Service Centers set up by the previous administration (and financed in part by fed-eral money). The Service Centers were neighborhood facilities with professional staffs borrowed from centrally located agencies (augmented by local nonprofessionals taken off the dole). They provided a multiplicity of social services under one roof *in the communities where they were needed.* They handled employment, vocational rehabilitation, various kinds of counseling services, etc., and they were located in Watts, Long Beach, and other such places which were remote in space and understanding from the cold, impersonal, bureaucratized central agencies designed for services of another era that is past.

The centers were important. They brought their services to the people, a matter of no little significance in a city like Los Angeles, which is spread out over 450 square miles with no effective transit other than the automobile—a convenience not always available to the poor. They were important in other ways too: they took people off the relief rolls. They gave jobs and dignity to the "neighborhood aides" through whom a normal and effective outreach was made to people in need who were not accessible to the office-bound professionals. Charles Sutton of the Long Beach *Press-Telegram,* who studied the effectiveness of the center in Long Beach, characterized the centers as "not waiting for people to come to them, but anticipating their needs and knocking on doors to help people help themselves."

Into the vacuum created by Governor Reagan's order to close the centers have rushed such hastily formed organizations as "The Citizens for Creative Welfare." CCW, led by a Negro militant named Ernest Preacely, is made up of community leaders and others who had once been so proud of the progress they were making in rebuilding the local people's confidence in themselves and their government after the burning issue of Watts. Now their strategy is to canvass every low-income neighborhood from door to door to pad the welfare rolls "with legitimate registrants to try to prove to the

Reagan Administration that it is cheaper to find jobs for people than to maintain them on relief."

How are the poor identified? The American poor have no faces. They are anonymous members of a statistical aggregate, who, if they receive a minimum number of dollars in income in a given year, qualify for poverty. What the minimum is enjoys a diversity of opinion. The poverty line is most often pegged at about $3,000 for a family of unspecified size. This is the figure originally recommended to the Johnson Administration by government economists for the President's War on Poverty. However, the obvious problem of applying a single figure to cover an infinite variety of cases arose inevitably. Are the families of a retired couple living alone, a farm family of four living in its own house and growing much of its own food, and a city family of six living in a rented apartment economically comparable? Obviously not. A recent study by Molly Orshansky of the Social Security Administration offers a more realistic approach to the recognition of poverty. In the Orshansky schedule, an individual living alone must have an income of at least $1,540 annually to meet his minimum needs. A family of four needs at least $3,130. A family of seven or more must have at least $5,090. These figures are all for non-farm families. The correlative requirements for farm families are reduced by 40 per cent on the supposition that the typical farmer grows a substantial amount of his food and does not pay rent on his house. The Orshansky approach, now used by the Office of Economic Opportunity, yields approximately the same *total* number of poor (34 million) as the flat $3,000 figure previously used by the Council of Economic Advisors (CEA) but distributes them differently. If the Orshansky index is used there are fewer poor farmers, more poor Negroes and children, and fewer aged persons who are poor. This change in the *identity* of the poor should of course have implications for tactics of alleviation.

But is poverty merely a matter of dollars and cents? In the late 1940's a family earning more than $2,000 a year was not considered poor. In 1957, $2,500 was enough to escape the stigma of poverty. Today $3,000 or more is required. Obviously the cost of living has gone up and the purchasing power of today's dollar is well below that of 1947. But it is equally true that living standards have changed, and conditions of existence which are associated with poverty today would not have seemed unusual a generation ago. Today a family may conceivably have electric lights, running water, even a TV set, and perhaps a jalopy of some sort and be considered "poor." This could hardly have been so in the 1920's, especially for rural families, where only one in a hundred enjoyed the luxury of electricity.

We must conclude, then, that poverty is at least in part culturally determined. In this society it is as much a level of existence relative to some cultural norm which has to do with generally available comforts and conveniences as it is an absolute which determines whether one lives or dies. Because of its relative nature, some economists like Victor Fuchs of the National Bureau of Economic Research advocate that any family with an income less than one-half of the national median family income should be considered poor.

But people do die from the effects of poverty, even in America. Despite the fact that we invest heavily in the provision of foods for the hungry all over the world—as indeed we should—about 2,000 Americans die annually from malnutrition directly associated with poverty. Thousands of others die for lack of proper medical care and from other causes in which poverty is a major factor. This suggests that poverty also functions independently of cultural norms.

The same people are not always poor. There is constant movement up *and* down across the line that separates the poor from the non-poor. But the *same kinds of people* are always at the bottom of the heap. We know that the aged, the ill, the very young, and the physically handicapped are peculiarly subject to poverty because of limitations of physical ability. But the lack of education, the possession of low or unmarketable skills, and racial discrimination are also major factors contributing to the poverty of millions of Americans. The poor, then, are those who are unable to participate in the productive process because their abilities are undiscovered, insufficient or obsolete, or because they are restricted or not considered because of racial prejudice.

Negroes constitute the largest single category of the poor in America because *all* the conditions which create poverty apply to them, with an ominous, interlocking circularity. Because it is an American tradition not to employ Negroes in certain categories of jobs, many Negroes who have marketable skills remain "undiscovered," and their potentials are wasted. Noting the inability of qualified Negroes to find work consistent with their qualification discourages motivation and encourages early school dropouts among Negro youths. These factors in turn produce low skills or *no* skills, adding to the general inability of the Negro subgroup to support itself in a society where jobs are competitive and race is an important factor in the competition.

Some civil rights leaders have finally begun to see that racial integration, which was mistakenly thought to be a first cause of social adjustment (from which all other derivative values would flow automatically), may well turn out to be a final cause which can only be fully realized through other approaches including economics. Dr. Whitney Young, the very able and perceptive Director of the National Urban League, has announced recently that the emphasis of his organization is geared more than ever to the production of "tangibles": tangible training, tangible jobs, tangible incomes. Such an approach makes sense for these times in America where in 1966

Negro unemployment reached 8.2 per cent—more than twice the white rate—and where (according to the U.S. Census Bureau) 57 per cent of all Negroes lived in substandard housing (as compared with 27 per cent of all whites). The picture may be even darker: two sociologists, Sidney M. Wilhelm and Edwin H. Powell, writing in a well-known sociological journal, say this of the American Negro:

> . . . he is not needed. He is not so much oppressed as unwanted; not so much unwanted as unnecessary; not so much abused as ignored. The dominant whites no longer need to exploit him. If he disappeared tomorrow he would hardly be missed. As automation proceeds, it is easier and easier to disregard him.[1]

Professors Wilhelm and Powell are not talking *only* about the Negro. Their diagnosis is presently more relevant to Negroes than to any other group, but by extension it applies to any group without skills, or with skills of diminishing marketability. They say "the Negro is merely a weather vane for the future. *His* experience will be a common one for many whites now deprived of some sort of usefulness. . . ."

More than 75 million Americans are presently employed, and the rate of unemployment is lower than at any time in nearly a decade. While we have more than 34 million people in poverty, the United States currently produces a total income which could provide $7,500 annually for each family. Our economy at its present level *could* provide a decent standard of living for us all. There is no excuse for widespread poverty in this society. While we preoccupy ourselves with the Jet Set, the Drug Set, and the Mini Set—who are themselves involved in a variety of escapes from the harshness and indifference of contemporary life—34 million people—right here in America—struggle to exist at all!

[1] Published in *Transaction* (Washington University, St. Louis).

It is anomalous that there is so much poverty, and more so that we know so little about it. We can *locate* it, if we wish— in the flats and tenements of the slums, and behind the ribbons of freeways that mark our cultural progress! But most of us regard it with a studied obliviousness. More disturbing is the fact that our experts don't seem to know really what it is, or how to measure it, or what to do about it, or how, or if it relates to the war in Vietnam. Scholars like Arthur Pearl at the University of Oregon associate poverty with a lack of opportunity—a lack of freedom of choice. The poor, he says, "are locked out of the chance to feel competent and important. . . . They are relegated to spectator roles." Pearl's solution is to train the poor in order to provide them with the necessary "credentials" to function in a "credential society."

Robert Theobald, the British socioeconomist (now living in New York), thinks that automation must inevitably eliminate jobs faster than we can create them. Mr. Theobald envisions a world without paid work, a leisure society made possible by a guaranteed annual income. But for the irascible Saul Alinsky, the gadfly organizer for community action, poverty is a matter of powerlessness. "People are poor because they lack the power to be non-poor." Hence, the poor must ally themselves in a struggle against the establishment which is the ordered, interlocking defensive machine of the rich.

Meanwhile, as the intellectual battle rages, and the War on Poverty strives valiantly against the odds, the rich get richer, the poor get poorer, and this Great Society stumbles on.

SOME THEOLOGICAL
AND ETHICAL IMPLICATIONS
OF THE BLACK GHETTO*

Ten years ago when I coined the name "Black Muslims" [1] and put together the companion phrase "Black Ghetto" [2] to more dramatically identify the Muslims' [1] social and geographical derivation, I could not have foreseen that I would someday be challenged to explain "theologically" and "ethically" what, in an endowed moment, I had created sociologically and journalistically. In the intervening years between then and now, "Black Ghetto," like "Black Muslim," has become a common phrase in the informal parlance of intergroup relations. As so used, it is generally (and I think, usefully) imprecise, but it carries a message that is seldom misunderstood: the black ghetto is where the Negroes live. With or without adjectival modification, if one is talking about America, "the ghetto" is where the Negroes live. "Black" is understood. In this country "ghetto" and "Negro" are reciprocally dependent. They go together. Find one and you have found the other.

Historically, of course, the ghetto has no special relation to black people. The ghetto is European in origin; but the *black*

---

* Published in *The Christian Century*, March 1, 1967.
[1] C. Eric Lincoln, *The Black Muslims in America* (Boston: Beacon Press, 1961), p. IV.
[2] *Ibid.*, p. 5.

ghetto is distinctively American. "The ghetto" as a generic phrase originated with the persecution of another minority—the Jews—and the present meaning of the word dates from the year 1516 when the Jews of the city of Venice were expelled from the general population and restricted to the Island of *Gheto*, the etymological archetype of all subsequent ghettos.[3] But unlike our black ghettos in America, the Jewish ghetto in early medieval Europe was at first a voluntary isolation, if not actually a right demanded for services rendered to the political establishments of the medieval cities of Europe.[4] To the devout Jews, ever conscious of The Promise of a unique, manifest destiny, there behind the invisible barriers that separated them from the alien cultures of their host societies, they would be safe from the strange, the distractive; and the fulfillment of The Promise could be pursued conscientiously even in the midst of a land not their own.

It is one of the bitterest ironies of history that this attempt at self-isolation was ultimately to cost the Jews across the succeeding centuries a fitfully continuing separation in extortion, terror, suffering, and death, and that the self-imposed isolation which was designed to minimize contacts and derivative antagonisms with the gentiles was ultimately to expose the Jews to every conceivable invention of human depravity. There is a lesson implicit in the Jewish experience which has been made explicit in the succeeding experiences of other minorities: people who live behind walls, voluntarily or involuntarily, sooner or later become the objects of suspicion and fear, anxiety and hatred. It makes no difference where the initiative for segregation originates—whether people wall themselves in or wall others out, or are themselves walled in by others. The day comes inevitably when the people behind the wall (or if you

[3] Eric Partridge, *Origins* (New York: The MacMillan Co., 1958), p. 253.
[4] George E. Simpson and J. Milton Yinger, *Racial and Cultural Minorities* (New York: Harper and Bros., 1958), p. 293.

prefer, beyond the pale) become the popular targets of those on the other side. The question of who built the wall and why becomes irrelevant. It is the existence of the wall itself that creates the suspicion and the hatred. "Something there is," said Robert Frost, "that doesn't love a wall."

Wherever men are shut away behind walls, visible or invisible, wherever artificial barriers restrict the natural flow of human intercourse and reduce the accessibility of individuals to each other, men raise the anguished question, *"What are they doing over there? What goes on beyond the wall?"* Who *are* those people? If we don't know them, their values, their dreams, their aspirations, and their behavior must somehow be less worthy than our own.

So it happened that the Jews who had segregated themselves in the interest of self-realization soon found themselves segregated against their will. The suspicions held against them are instructive: "They had tails; they had a special odor 'over and above the all-pervading unwashed odor of medieval humanity.' They were supposed to sacrifice Christian children, using their blood in Passover rites . . . they got hold of sacred bread —the eucharistic body of Christ—and tortured it until it bled." [5]

The ghetto was in the making. It began in the minds of men:

> There was a transition from voluntary to involuntary segregation. By the time of the Crusades, the [Christian] Church was restricting contact, for fear the alien beliefs of the Jews would weaken the faith of the Christians. "The Lateran Council of 1179 definitely forbade true believers to lodge among the infidels, lest they be contaminated by false belief." [6]

By 1555 the pointer had come full circle. In that year Pope Paul IV decreed that Jews were "henceforth to be segregated

[5] *Ibid.*, p. 293.
[6] Simpson and Yinger, *op. cit.*, pp. 293–94.

strictly in their own quarter, which was to be surrounded by a high wall and provided with gates, closed at night." [7]

The Negroes in the United States never did want to be isolated from the mainstream of the American experience. If they ever thought of themselves as having a manifest destiny, it was inevitably conceived as being part and parcel of the common destiny of the American homeland. If theirs had been an ancient culture worthy of veneration and preservation—and who can argue that it was not?—250 years of chattel slavery, 250 years of total isolation from that native culture had dimmed their memories. They could no longer remember the ancient places, the shrines, the cities, the mountains, and the rivers that were sacred to their fathers. They could not recall the ancient names—the tribes, the families, the great warriors, the holy men, the feast days, the laws, and the customs, the rites, the very gods which would have given them identity in a society where they were doomed to be invisible men. They had forgotten the words—the language without which they could not reconstruct their past or hope for a future that could be ethnically or culturally distinctive. No, the Negro in America opted to become what the centuries had best prepared him to be: American. That the white American has not even yet learned to accept him as such, a hundred years after the legal fact, is an enlightening commentary on the status of race relations and Christian conscience in this country.

The fact that every city in this country which has more than a handful of Negroes has also a black ghetto suggests on the face of it a rather controlled suppression of the democratic spirit, and an implicit affirmation of the power and presence of a pervasive evil which divides men on the arbitrary basis of color and which seeks to deny them the normal right of

[7] J. O. Hertzler, in Isague Graeber and S. H. Britt (ed.), *Jews in a Gentile World* (New York: The MacMillan Co., 1942), p. 72.

free and meaningful association. Twenty-four hundred years ago Aristotle observed that man is a social animal. If he had been an anthropologist as well as a philosopher, he might have made the further observation that in the absence of arbitrary constraint, social intercourse is not inhibited by racial factors. The evidences we see throughout the world, and most particularly in the United States, are overwhelming. Since the very beginning of civilization the natural tendency of the human species has been toward interpenetration and interassimilation, although no generation has been without its Stoddard, its Hitler, its Verwoerd, its Rockwell, or its George Wallace. There are no pure races: none that are pure in blood, and none that are pure in heart. Because this is so, the arbitrary separation and alienation of men on the basis of skin color is a fraudulent consuetude perpetrated against society by sick men with delusions of their own self-importance, or who shrink from the challenge to love thy neighbor. . . . A man who is small-minded and insecure can never love a stranger, but then, when he sets up artificial barriers to the possibility of friendship, he narrows the range of his love-potential to a mere handful of individuals enough like himself to provide reinforcement for an ego that is weak and uncertain. Such a man is caught in a vicious circle of truncated emotions: he cannot love anyone who is not like himself, because he does not permit himself to know at a meaningful level anyone who is not like himself. And he does not permit himself to know a stranger lest that stranger prove himself worthy of the love he is unprepared to extend to him.

This is the fundamental evil of the black ghetto. It separates, segregates, and alienates people who are of one faith, one culture, one God, and one destiny; and so frequently, I might add, one blood. It divides people who logically belong together in the sense that they share common goals and common values, whose pasts are bracketed together by three and a half centuries of interlocking experiences, and whose futures are one future together, or no future at all. The black ghetto by its very existence degrades and debases the people who live in it, and it provides for its creators a false sense of their personal worth which may be entirely unrelated to any objective criteria. The black ghetto is the modern expression of an anachronistic racial tribalism which conceives as exotic any person not cast in the monochromatic mold of the moment's racial establishment.

The Negro in America did not elect to live in the black ghetto. He does not want to live in the black ghetto, or any other ghetto. Anyone who says he is happy there, or wants to be there, is, in the kindest terms I am able to employ here, misinformed. For the *black ghetto* is more than a place: it is a condition. The black ghetto is not just a slum, although a slum may be and frequently is the physical location of the ghetto. But the two may be differentiated: A slum is a deteriorated part of the city where the housing, recreational facilities, and municipal services such as garbage collection, lighting, and police protection are substandard. People may, and do, move out of slums, and people of any race may, and do, live in them. The black ghetto is a section of the city which has *enforced* boundaries, visible or invisible, which shut in the people of one race and minimize their contacts with the larger society as effectively as did the island community of the original ghetto, or the walls of Paul IV. It may be a horrible slum like much of New York's Harlem or Chicago's South Side, or it may be a "golden ghetto" like Atlanta's Collier Heights—complete with swimming pools, split-level houses, manicured lawns and terraces. But it is a black ghetto all the same, and the people who live there are deprived of normal access to the full continuum of values consistent with their rights as citizens and human beings.

The blacks entrapped in the modern ghetto escape from it

only with the greatest difficulty, for the concept of the all-white neighborhood as a necessary and desirable prerogative of the white race is deeply entrenched in the prevailing sentiments of this society and is reinforced by practically every institution which relates to this society directly or indirectly. The deeper tragedy is that the same sentiments that conceive the black ghetto as a proper residential reservation for blacks conceive and enforce other reservations in employment, education, religious life, and the administration of justice. Racism is like hydrophobia: you can't have just a little of it. And racism is the characteristic condition of this society. The black ghetto is but one of the evidences of its power and pervasiveness.

Racism distorts, nay in many cases precludes the interpersonal relationships which make for a sound community whether one's point of reference is sociological or theological. Spatial propinquity—i.e., physical nearness or accessibility—is the essential condition for the articulation of social roles by means of which common attitudes, values, and group identity become possible.[8] Whatever inhibits social interaction is dysfunctional to group maintenance or the stability of the community, for "frequency of interaction is associated with people's attractiveness and accommodation to one another, and common conceptions . . . are developed and reinforced."[9] This reinforcement is what Emile Durkheim calls " 'moral density,' a consistency of viewpoint, a uniformity in the cultural fabric that enhances group solidarity."[10] In short, the existence of the black ghetto is inimical to any possibility of producing a unity of spirit, a sharing of values, a mutual commitment to a unitary moral code. How then, while we are

[8] See Everett K. Wilson, *Sociology* (Homewood, Ill.: The Dorsey Press, 1966), p. 272.
[9] *Ibid.*
[10] *Ibid.*

raising pious hymns of praise and adulation, dare we stand
aghast at the anguished cry of "Burn! Baby, Burn!" that
wells up from the stinking bowels of the ghetto? This laby-
rinthine nether world of dying dreams and living frustration,
unilluminated by hope and unwarmed by love, is of *our* creation. *We* built the walls. Is it really so surprising that in their
desperation the denizens of the ghetto seek to burn them
down? If the idea is monstrous to us, can it be because we
know what they do not know: the walls of the black ghetto
cannot be destroyed by fire. After the holocaust they are
higher, more invisible, more impenetrable than before.

In the *City of God* St. Augustine reminds us that to deter-
mine the quality of a nation you must discover what the people cherish. If, as it seems we may, we cherish the accident of
color above all else, there is a real question as to whether we
possess the moral qualities which can produce the peculiar
stamina which might make possible our survival under the
various stresses which impinge increasingly upon our civilization. We have been slumbering fitfully behind the dubious protection of a doctrine we know in our hearts to be both false and
cynical, namely that our mere possession of the Judeo-Chris-
tian heritage is in itself a manifest evidence of what we are,
or at the very least, of what we are striving to become. But
behind the satirical façades of our cumbersome pronounce-
ments we continue to pursue the most vicious idolatry.

John Bennett is speaking to a spurious self-image of this
generation when he admonishes us that "no degree of depth
in theology and no degree of warmth in piety can compensate
for . . . social insensitivity."[11] His words are wasted because
if we had either depth . . . or warmth . . . we could hardly be
insensitive to the legitimate needs for self-expression of those
around us. Emil Brunner says that we are "persons in commu-

[11] John Bennett, *Christian Ethics and Social Policy* (New York: Charles
Scribner's Sons, 1946), p. 3.

nity." We are not things to be manipulated or objects to be observed. The human personality fulfills its potential development or is mutilated and deformed in terms of what we do to others and what others do to us.[12]

In a society such as ours where the religious community claims to be coextensive with the political or social community, the existence of the black ghetto is theologically and morally unjustified, just as it has been shown to be socially dysfunctional. Politically speaking, men form communities to pursue their mutual advantages. Hence, at the purely human level it is self-interest that brings men together and sustains them in a social equilibrium. But the religious community derives not from the self-interest of man but from an act of divine love expressed as the will of God. It would seem to follow that the Christian community provides the optimum possibility for the growth and development of all its members. It cannot be a segregated community, for as Paul lays it down in his letter to the Romans: none of us lives to himself, or dies to himself.[13] "We are," he says to the Ephesians, "members one of another."[14] We are a community of persons bound together under God through the instrumentality of love. The community we share, says Joseph Haroutuniam, "is a free association by virtue of a common deliverance and a common covenant with God."[15]

The promotion of self-interest leads men to distrust the wisdom of God in his establishment of the beloved community. They substitute their limited judgment for his omniscience, and because their faith in the grand strategy of God is weak and irresolute, they play at little strategies to remedy

[12] See Albert K. Rasmussen, *Christian Social Ethics* (Englewood Cliffs, N.J.: Prentice-Hall, 1956), p. 28.
[13] Romans 14:7.
[14] Ephesians 4:25.
[15] See Richard J. Spann (ed.), *The Church and Social Responsibility* (New York: Abingdon Press, 1953), pp. 42 and 43.

what God forgot. Albert Rasmussen catches the spirit of the true Christian role when he defines the Christian ethic as "an ethic to end all ethics . . . a faith that asks not for specific deeds but for the self-surrender of man to a total new active orientation of his whole self toward God and the consequent relation of outgoing concern toward his neighbors. Then," says Dr. Rasmussen, "man's responses to his fellowmen and toward his ethical decisions begin to take on a new quality of openness to the needs of neighbor and to the continuous transformation under God." [16] In short, the true Christian must be willing to stand on his faith in the context of community. He must be aware that God orders the community and is at work in it, gathering together through love *all* men against the sure and certain coming of his kingdom.

What Christian, then, knowing all men to be alienated from God, and knowing God to be at work in reconciliation—what Christian, then, will seek to work a double alienation by excluding from the community of human kind *any* child of God? Better it would be for such a man that he wrap himself in the sick-clothes of his own bigotry and exclude *himself* from the beloved community. For if any man be unfit to sit in the councils of human deliberation under the judgment of God, he is the man!

The black ghetto could not exist in a just society, for it abrogates the rights and the responsibilities of those restricted by it. S. Paul Schilling defines a right as "a claim which belongs to every man as a member of the human family." Without rights, no individual can become what he is capable of becoming. A right implies a freedom, for according to Professor Schilling, "a freedom is the opportunity to exercise a right." Rights and freedom together give meaning to responsibility, for a responsibility is equivalent to a duty. It is "an

[16] Rasmussen, *op. cit.*, p. 67.

instance of accountability," [17] for something within the control of an individual or of persons acting in concert. Rights
and responsibilities are theogenetic. They derive from man's
relationship to God made manifest through Jesus Christ. Man
is created in the image of God and is called upon to fulfill
whatever responsibilities there are inherent in being the son of
God. Every man, not some only, is an end in himself, not a
means—not an instrument for the realization of the selfish,
egocentric ends of another. Men are of equal worth and dignity. If they are to realize their unique potentialities, fulfilling
the promise inherent in the image of God, they must as a
minimum enjoy the freedom without which there can be no
responsibility.

Justice, according to Aristotle, is of two kinds: distributive
and retributive. Distributive justice protects the rights of a person to his share of whatever values there are to distribute at a
given time within a given social order. Retributive justice re-
fers to administration to enforce obedience of the law.[18] In a
racist society which maintains a thousand racial ghettos,
neither kind of justice would seem to be in vogue. "Without
justice," said Augustine, "what are realms but great robber
bands?" This, in other language, is precisely the cry of the
contemporary poor behind the invisible barriers in America.
C. H. McIlwain's commentary on Augustine is instructive:
"Justice and justice alone," said he, "is the only possible bond
that can unite men as a true populus in a real *res publica*." [19]

Again I must refer to the *Ethics* of Aristotle, where it is
said that "Justice is equality . . . quite apart from any argument." Hence it is unjust for the society, or for the state, or

---

[17] Spann, *op. cit.*, p. 12.
[18] Cf. Walter G. Muelder, *Foundations of the Responsible Society* (New
York: Abingdon Press, 1959), p. 91.
[19] C. H. McIlwain, *The Growth of Political Thought in the West* (New
York: The MacMillan Co., 1932), p. 158.

for any ruling hegemony to impoverish the lives of free citizens materially, esthetically, or otherwise, by holding them to a level below that which some members at least might well attain by their own efforts.[20] John Stuart Mill declared that "there is something which it is right to do, and which some individual has a right to have done. Justice implies something which it is not only right to do and wrong not to do, but which some individual person can claim from us as his moral right." [21]

The black ghetto is the monstrous symbol of our mutual distrust. The perpetuation of the ghetto, its cultivation and defense, is an extraordinary act of racial conceit and social irresponsibility. Beyond that, it is a contemptuous disregard for Christian ethics and social justice. Immanuel Kant thought men ought to be free because they are moral beings. And he thought the ideal community could exist because men are rational. Reason he supposed to be the "cohesive force that empowers us to share purposes, to respect one another and to work together for good." [22] Reason is an alternative to coercion. It "demands that we adopt the perspectives of other men, and that we treat others, like ourselves, with justice." [23]

As far as the eradication of the black ghetto is concerned, we do not, at this time, seem to be moving toward either reason or justice. Rather, we seem intent on justification. Our present policy seems to be to maintain the ghetto, but to gild it with new schools and high-rise tenements in the hope that, being physically more commodious, it will be psychologically less obnoxious. I doubt that such will satisfy the yearnings of black people to be free—free of the barriers that set them aside

[20] William K. Frankens in Richard B. Brandt (ed.), *Social Justice* (Englewood Cliffs, N.J.: Prentice-Hall, 1952), p. 14.

[21] *Ibid.*, p. 7.

[22] Robert T. Harris, *Social Ethics* (Philadelphia: J. B. Lippincott Co., 1962), p. 98.

[23] *Ibid.*, p. 98.

from the American mainstream. George Washington once re-
marked of the black slaves being imported into America: "I
fear that this will become a troublesome species of property
before many generations have passed over our heads." As it
turns out, Mr. Washington was right—but not necessarily so.
So long as black Americans are conceived as "property" and
manipulated as "things," so long *will* they be "troublesome."
In the interest of peace, the promotion of justice, and the
recognition of a common Father, a common heritage, and a
common destiny, perhaps we could now with profit consider
the possibility that what once was property to the mind of
man is now people by the grace of God.

COLOR AND GROUP IDENTITY
IN THE UNITED STATES*

> Mary had a little lamb,
> Its fleece was white as snow,
> And everywhere that Mary went
> That little white lamb could go.
>
> Mary had another lamb,
> Its fleece was black, you see,
> They thought he was a "you-know-what"
> And hung him from a tree.[1]

   In the United States where the enduring problem in social relations is between whites and Negroes, skin color is probably the most important single index for uncritical human evaluation. It is paradoxical that this is so, for color is notoriously unreliable as a tool for determining any substantial qualities of an individual, particularly his "race." And it is with race that the question of color is ultimately concerned. Despite this obvious unreliability, color is made to function as a cultural index for racial determination whenever it is conceived of as a valid external symbol of supposedly intrinsic qualities. The presence or absence of these qualities determines whether a person belongs to an "inferior" or "superior" social group and

---

* Published in *Daedalus*, Spring, 1967.
[1] From "Joe Jipson," in "The Autobiography of a Southern Town," an unpublished manuscript by C. Eric Lincoln.

whether his life chances are circumscribed or maximized in terms of his group membership.

In social relations in the United States color is often read as a signal to denigrate, to discriminate, to segregate. It takes on the characteristics of a cultural norm, so much so that a complex of rewards, punishments, and the strictest taboos have grown up around it. American children, both Negro and white, very early develop behavior patterns and adopt value systems based on color, and American adults are seldom free from its connotations. That a racial determination on the basis of color can only be approximate and for a limited spectrum of individuals at best does not seem to impair its credibility as a legitimate index for human evaluation. Nor does it seem to diminish the apparent *need* for identifying persons by race. On the surface this would seem to indicate that America's cultural concern about color is essentially nominal. The need to make decisions on a racial basis is perhaps psychologically atavistic, a tribal anachronism rooted in the dim past when everyone not a member of the tribe threatened its well-being.

Thousands of Negroes "pass" permanently into the white race each year. This cannot be effectively prevented so long as there are interracial unions, with or without benefit of law or clergy. Thousands of others pass whenever it provides social or economic opportunities not readily available outside the majority group. Reliable estimates on the basis of three hundred and fifty years of miscegenation and passing suggest that there are several million "Caucasians" in this country who are part Negro insofar as they have Negro blood or Negro ancestry.[2] Since there are few Negro Americans who do not have some white blood, the continuing preoccupation with racial identification by color would seem to be of little reward

[2] Sociologist Robert P. Stuckert of Ohio State University estimates: "Over 28 million white persons are descendants of persons of African origins"— about 21 per cent of the Caucasian population of the United States.

—the more crucial facts having already been established by a countervailing proclivity.

Nonetheless, American society has troubled itself considerably to detect by various supplementary devices—sometimes refined, but more often of a cruder sort—what may be undetectable to the uncritical eye. It thus reaffirms its apparent need (and the quality of its commitment) for the establishment of racial identity as a crucial factor in social intercourse. A generation ago when strict segregation followed identification, some of the night clubs, hotels, and other places of entertainment and public accommodation in Chicago and other cities hired "spotters" to point out light-skinned Negroes who sought to pass for white and enter the segregated establishments. Since the operating premise of the white proprietors was that "one coon can recognize another," the spotters were always Negroes, some of whom were themselves light enough to pass. The system broke down during the depression years when few Negroes, light-skinned or otherwise, had enough money to bother about trying to spend it in places where they had to run a color gauntlet. Having nobody to spot, the "spotters" felt their jobs in jeopardy and began to ask their friends to come by occasionally in the interest of the survival of the profession. The whole sordid arrangement collapsed when the supply of friends of "passable" skin color ran low and the ersatz "Caucasians" became darker and darker with hair that was fuzzier and fuzzier. Reduced to spotting the obvious, the spotters were soon dispensed with.

This absurd practice demonstrates the near pathological obsession with race and color Americans have exhibited. It is *e pluribus unum*—one out of a multitude. In the illustration given, those most anxious about color and identity were Caucasian, which is to say, white. But in a well-known Southern city a leading Negro church for years discouraged the attendance of would-be worshipers who were darker than a *café au lait* stripe painted conveniently on the doorjamb of the sanctuary.

In its American manifestations, the fundamental problem of color and group identity derives in large measure from the desire of the established white hegemony, particularly the former slave-owning class, to distinguish itself by all means available from the blacks, who, whether as slaves or freedmen, had little status and no power.[3] As long as the vast majority of the blacks were of unmixed African descent, the problem was minimized. Their distinctive visibility made their racial origins unmistakable. In fact, the very first significance of color was the early development of a rationale in the colonies that made it possible to hold a black bond servant for life, to make him a slave, while a white bond servant could be held only for a term of years.[4]

From the date that blacks could, as a matter of course, be held in legal servitude for life, color became an important index of race, and hence of prestige and status.[5] A ban against intermarriage was immediately instituted. Theretofore intermarriage between black bondsmen from Africa and white bondmaids from England and Ireland had been common.

---

[3] In a larger sense, the problem of color and identity in America is related to the general ascendancy of the West, which is to say white Europeans, since the fifteenth century, and the subsequent colonization of Asia, Africa, and the New World. In his book, *Caste, Class and Race* ([Garden City, N.Y., 1948], p. 346), Oliver Cox makes the signal observation that "since the belief in white superiority—that is to say white nationalism—began to move over the world, no people of color have been able to develop race prejudice independent of whites."

[4] See John Hope Franklin, *From Slavery to Freedom* (New York, 1947), p. 70 ff.

[5] This was first practiced in Virginia in 1661; Maryland followed in 1663. A Virginia law of 1670 fixed the status of Negroes and Indians respectively by decreeing that "all servants not being Christians" (that is, not being "white") coming into the colony by sea, "shall be slaves for their lives." Those "coming by land" (Indians) could be bound for a term of years.

Social acceptability was measured in terms of class, which could be transcended, rather than in terms of race, which was immutable. In the context of a distribution of status and power that implied the freedom of all white men and the susceptibility to chattel slavery of all Negroes, color became the visual rule of thumb for the assignment of "place" or status.

It is no less ironic for all its inevitability that Negroes, who were (and who remain) the prime subjects of color discrimination, adopted color as an index of social worth. They made the evaluative modifications necessary to suit their peculiar condition as a color caste undergirding an otherwise class-oriented society.

In the process of establishing a "democracy" in the New World, colonial Europeans did not contemplate the inclusion of Negroes (or Indians for that matter) in the ruling caste. As American social and moral philosophy evolved through an agonizing assessment of economic preferments and political demands, consensus arose that the issue of color and caste implied in Negro slavery should be excluded from the founding documents of the emergent democracy.[6] For the British founders and the succeeding generations of Euro-Americans, the issue of color was without complication once Negro slavery had become institutionalized. Indeed, the issue of political status transcended the issue of color. All white men were free; all black men were slaves (with the exception of "free" Negroes who were in a sort of limbo in between).[7]

[6] The Continental Congress refused to accept Thomas Jefferson's draft of the Declaration of Independence which included a strong indictment of Negro slavery and of the English Crown which was allegedly responsible for the establishment and continuation of slavery in the colonies. It is significant that once free of British rule, the colonies continued slavery on their own, although there was always dissent against the practice.

[7] "His color," says Wade, "suggested servitude, but his national status secured a portion of freedom." Richard C. Wade, *Slavery in the Cities* (New York: Oxford University Press, 1964), p. 249.

Unlike the complicated experiments of slaveholding countries that sought to match a hierarchy of privileges with a spectrum of color, America's color caste arrangement was inflexible. There were but two recognized categories of color: "white" and "colored." "Colored" was the common designation for any person having any Negro ancestry whatever—no matter how "light" or how "dark" his skin color, and irrespective of any quantity of "white blood" less than 100 per cent. The term *mulatto* was loosely used in commercial parlance to refer to a slave of mixed blood in any degree, but it had no political, social, or legal meaning. From the perspective of the white ruling caste, *all* Negroes of *any* color were of a lower caste. The question of color as a matter of identity was to have substantial meaning only to Negroes.

In the search for an identity based on color, the Negro reacted (and perhaps is still reacting) to a status first ascribed to him by the white man and then perpetuated in a self-fulfilling prophecy. The white man rationalized the Negro's peculiar fitness, even his God-willed destiny, to be a slave and then enslaved him. The Negro in his yearnings to be free and equal, and everywhere observing that blacks were in servitude and whites were free, mistakenly equated whiteness as a necessary corollary to freedom and blackness as the inevitable concomitant to bondage.

> Aught's de aught
> Figger's de figger . . .
> All fo' de white man
> And none fo' de nigger.

Even the experience of emancipation, a rather qualified freedom, did not significantly change the black man's awe of the mystery of whiteness.

There is not, to my knowledge, any history of pre-colonial color-consciousness among the various African tribes whose descendants make up the Negro population in America. If color-consciousness was *not* a factor in their social relations, two hundred and fifty years of slavery, and another hundred years of marginal involvement in the pervasive, ubiquitous culture of a white, European society, have created a color-consciousness that has become such a factor. In a sub-society alienated so completely and with such finality from its parent culture and its traditional spectrum of values, a modified adoption of the cultural values of the host society would seem to be predictable.

At the uncritical stage of their yearning for equivalence, the powerless and the disinherited find attractive whatever is associated with the peculiar mystique of the group in power. This was true of the Jews, the American colonists, and probably of every other subject people. The slave affects the style of his master; the student, the language of his teacher. Whether the quality affected or yearned after is germane to the status associated with it is unimportant so long as it is *thought* to be by those impressed by it. In America the white man was unchallenged in his power. His grand style bespoke wealth and learning. Negroes were powerless, poor, and ignorant. Indeed, both races commonly supposed that an unmixed Negro was incapable of education, to say nothing of mastering the intricacies of politics or economics.

If the secret of the white man's success lay in his color, it stood to reason that the closer to being "white" a black man was, the more likely he was to have power and status. This reasoning was reinforced by the slave-era tradition of making household servants of the slavemaster's mulatto offspring, thus securing them in positions of relative privilege *vis-à-vis* the unmixed field hands. Frequently, the law permitting, a conscience-stricken master would free the half-white fruit of his cabin dalliances when they reached majority, or he would provide for their freedom in his will.

Thus a substantial proportion of free Negroes were mulattoes. The various literary and mutual-aid societies, and sometimes churches formed by "free persons of color," [8] often disdained the admission of free Negroes with dark skin. When the slavocracy was destroyed and all Negroes were elevated to a single legal status, the Negro group—as a sub-society—already had an emerging class arrangement based on color within a nether caste also defined by color. The mulattoes were the top of the lowly heap. They maintained their position as a class within the caste until after World War II when values like wealth, education, and profession reduced the mere possession of a light skin to relative insignificance.

Yet to say that color is dead as an aspect of racial psychosis would be to lay prematurely to rest a troublesome syndrome likely to defy interment. Quite apart from its elemental concern with status and power, color as a cultural value has continuing significance for aesthetics and for personal identity. The prevailing conceptions of what or who is beautiful vary widely between native Africans and their Afro-American counterparts. The white ideal of feminine pulchritude, though less stressed than formerly, is still the archetype for the overwhelming majority of Negro-American women and the persistent choice of Negro men. Cosmetic preparations for lightening skin and straightening hair represent a multimillion-dollar market among Negroes not favored with Caucasoid features. Among the less affluent and more credulous, urine rinses for the face and "mammy-leg" [9] presses for the hair contribute to the unending search for some approximation of the white ideal.

[8] A term normally meaning "colored"—that is, "Negro."
[9] A sort of cap made from a woman's stocking, the "mammy-leg" is much used by males and females to hold the hair in place during informal hours at home. They are sometimes seen on children and teen-agers on neighborhood streets.

To the intense delight of a street-corner gathering, a Negro punster described the ideal woman in exaggerated terms reflecting the Negro's preoccupation with color:

> She got to be white, Jack—
> 'Cause white is right
> Both day and night!
> She got to be old and white,
> 'Cause if she's old
> She's been white longer!
> She got to be big and white,
> Cause if she's big
> She's much more white!
> But listen, Jack—
> If she just can't be white
> Then let her be real light brown! [10]

A college jester put it this way: "A light woman is your passport to Negro society. I'd rather give a light woman plane fare to St. Louis than to tell a tack head [11] what time the train leaves!"

During the uncertain years of World War II, "passport parties" were actually held as pranks on some college campuses. To attend such a party, male escorts were made to pay (unknown to their dates) a color tax based on the complexion of the girls they escorted; the money thus raised made up a pot to buy refreshments. Any girl as fair as a secretly agreed upon "Fairy Queen" was designated a "Natural Passport"; she and her escort were admitted without charge. The color of the male was inconsequential. That college youths could face the color issue squarely enough to joke about it is probably indicative of its declining importance as early as two decades ago, but is no less indicative of its pervasiveness.

[10] C. Eric Lincoln, "Joe Jipson," in "The Autobiography of a Southern Town."
[11] A slang term for a dark woman with crimpy hair.

The problem of negative associations with blackness goes deeper than aesthetics. American culture associates Negroes with darkness, an extremely negative quality. In the innocent and painful prattle of Negro children heard a scant generation ago, *"Black is evil!"* was a retort intended to account for behavior one disapproved of in a playmate.[12] In the rural areas black people were frequently associated with sorcery and voodoo.[13] Everywhere black people were pitied, for deep in the soul of even the whitest Negro was an erosive *self*-pity, even a self-hatred that gnawed at his vitals, questioned his manhood, and excused his failures in a way he did not want them to be excused. There was something inherent in being black that marked a man, something sinister that mocked a man.

The crucial question has always been the question of identity. Who *is* this Negro whose identifying characteristic is his color and what is his status in the world? *Whence does that status derive?* Is he African—an involuntary expatriate? Is he, in fact, "just a nigger"—a monster, blackened by God, broken in servitude, and inherently incapable of human excellence? How should he designate himself? By what name should he identify himself before the world and serve notice of what he conceives himself to be?

There has been little unanimity in the Negro's search for his identity. The Negro slaves came from many tribes and many cultures. Even though the experience of slavery reduced them all to a common denominator, it did not fuse them into an ideological unit. Only attractive ideas and persuasive lead-

12 In Boston, the author was once physically attacked by a white child with no other explanation than, "I don't like you because you're black!"

13 A belief possibly reinforced by once popular "jungle" films and stories; but possibly a recollection of a fragmentary cultural experience having to do with tribal religious rites or witchcraft.

ership could do that; the nature of slavery in America left little room for the development of either.

The confusion of identity is vividly expressed in the names Negroes have chosen at various times to designate themselves: "persons of color," "colored people," "Negroes," "colored Americans," "black Anglo-Saxons," "Americans," "Afro-Americans," "Afra-Americans," "Negro Americans"; and, more recently: "black men," "black Americans," "black people." Widely used by white writers, but commonly rejected by Negro intellectuals and black nationalists, is the term *American Negroes.* This eristical term allegedly carries the stamp of something "made in America" and is the inverse of the designations commonly applied to other ethnic groups— "German Americans," for instance.[14] "That we are called 'American Negroes,'" a prominent Negro writer has said, "is a concession of courtesy on the part of our Caucasian brothers. In translation, the 'American Negro' can only mean 'our niggers.'"

Despite some improvements in the Negroes' position as a major ethnic group pressing for a larger share of the common values of the society, the question of color and identity has in some sense become more involved and more intricate than before. There have been changes in the way Caucasians and Negroes see each other, and profound changes in the way Negroes see themselves. These newly developing attitudes have not always found mutual acceptance, nor are they necessarily consistent with one another. The de-escalation of color as an index of social standing in the Negro sub-society immeasurably strengthened and unified the factions previously contending for leadership and prestige. Forced to more dili-

14 The implication, say the critics, is that the Negro has no prior nationality or culture, that he is in fact a creation of the white man, "something made in America." Only the Indian should have "American" placed before his ethnic name, it is argued.

gently prepare themselves, the descendants of the less-favored field hands of plantation days have at least caught up. Today education, wealth, high social status, and leadership are distributed fairly evenly across the color spectrum of the Negro community.

If anything, the light-skinned Negro is at a disadvantage. In the old days color meant (at least nominal) privilege, for it bespoke the presence of the master's blood. Today, as the Negro develops an increasing appreciation of his own accomplishments and shares vicariously the accomplishments of other non-whites, the premium on "the master's blood" is signally diminished. Anyone whose light skin color is thought to be of recent derivation is exposed to a degree of censure and disapproval not known in former times.

As far as the larger society is concerned, the presence of white blood in a Negro does not bridge the chasm between castes any more today than it did formerly. In personal relations Caucasians have, since the plantation days, usually been less threatened by blacks who were thought of as "knowing their places" than by mulattoes or "yellow niggers" who were always suspect. This white attitude can be explained in part, of course, by guilt feelings deriving from a covert recognition of kinship, which could never be openly admitted without violating the strictest taboos. But there was also the deep-seated belief that too much white blood transformed the stereotyped docile, accommodating Negro into a dissatisfied, potential troublemaker. Hence, enduring bonds of affection and qualified respect frequently developed between whites and darker Negroes, a felicitous relationship from which light-skinned Negroes were generally excluded. In quite recent times this tradition has undergone some interesting changes that reflect the inconsistencies of a color differential.

When civil rights legislation first required the employment

of Negroes in major industry wherever possible the "instant Negroes" [15] hired were of very fair complexions. Negroes serving as clerks and saleswomen in department stores or as route salesmen were frequently mistaken for white by their customers and sometimes by their co-workers. This was, of course, precisely what their employers had hoped for. In hiring Negroes who could "pass," they complied with the law without appearing to have done so. They thus reduced the supposed threat of customer and white employee reaction against being served by or working with Negroes. This policy was discontinued in favor of hiring highly visible Negroes and placing them in the most conspicuous assignments when compliance officials could discover no change in hiring policies, and Negro leaders protested that their followers wanted to "see their people on the job without having to look for them."

There are signs that the civil rights movement as a supporting thrust to a certain degree of Negro "readiness" in terms of education, accomplishment, and demonstrated potential has successfully breached the wall separating Negroes and whites into two castes. The breach is certainly not general, but for the first time in American history Negroes enjoy some degree of lateral mobility. There is *some* social movement across color lines. Perhaps the sudden recognition of this fact contributed in no small degree to the amazing "pull-back" on the part of large numbers of whites who had been heavily involved in the civil rights movement so long as it was limited to civil rights—and concentrated in the South. The white retreat would seem to buttress other evidence that white America in general, despite some fits and starts, is not yet ready to accept Negroes on equal terms so long as they remain Negroes. Arnold Toynbee's observations of thirty years ago are still valid:

[15] Negroes hired in token numbers merely to comply with the law.

> The . . . [Negro] may have found spiritual salvation in the
> White Man's faith; he may have acquired the White Man's
> culture and learnt to speak his language with the tongue of
> an angel; he may have become adept in the White Man's eco-
> nomic technique, and yet it profits him nothing if he has not
> changed his skin.[16]

A few select, individual Negroes have been able to approach
the American mainstream with varying degrees of marginality. In doing so, they run the inevitable risk of becoming as
alienated from the nether culture from which they came as
they are likely to remain in reference to the culture they seek
to enter. But change *is* occurring.

Even as the machinery of caste is being dismantled and dis-
carded, the color-caste psychology persists. It is not difficult
to understand the continuing frustrations of the black masses.
A universal system of apartheid has, in effect, been exchanged
for a selective system of apartheid. This may be progress, but
it is not progressive enough to satisfy the present-day needs
of the black millions who are still beyond the pale. The color
computer has been programmed to extend to selected Negroes
of high accomplishment selected categories of privileges previously withheld from all Negroes. An "integrated" society in
which the common values of that society will be freely accessible to the general population regardless of color has not been
realized, nor does it seem to be rapidly approaching.

Taking no comfort from what they perceive as an *entente
cordiale* between the white establishment and the Negro leadership class, the black *lumpen proletariat* seethes with hostility
and resentment. Despite modifications of law and practice
produced by the efforts of the civil rights movement, the
black masses are unimpressed because they are unaffected.

[16] Arnold J. Toynbee, *A Study of History*, Vol. 1 (London, Oxford University Press, 1935), p. 224.

Critical selectivity functions at the top; the tortured masses at the bottom feel no tremor of change.

The Great Society has spent millions of dollars in the interest of the poor and the disinherited. In doing so, the government created yet another clique of petty bureaucrats and interposed them between the people and the help they need. By day the black ghetto is resplendent with sleek, fat professionals—Negro and white—striving mightily to remold the people in images they reject and despise; by night—the professionals having fled home to the suburbs—the people gather on the street corners to contemplate the probabilities of black power or the ecstasy of long, hot summers. Despite the ministrations of the professionals, the people are as hungry, as unemployed, and as hostile as before.

As their frustrations multiply, the black masses become more and more alienated from the larger society and from the tiny Negro middle class that hopes to cross the chasm eventually and to enter the American mainstream. The problem of color and identity takes on crucial meaning in this context. The term *Negro*, which has for so long aroused mixed emotions among those who accepted it, has for the militant [17] masses become an epithet reserved for the Negro middle class, particularly those suspected of desiring to be integrated into the white society.

Neither the traditional black nationalists nor the advocates of "black power," which is a new form of militant black nationalism, accept integration as being either possible or desirable under existing conditions. Integration is interpreted as a one-way street. It means to those not impressed by its possibilities the abandonment of traditional values and styles of life on the off chance of being accepted by a group "which

[17] The greater portion of the black masses can still be classified as "quiescent," although they are certainly more susceptible to sporadic activities than ever before.

never appreciated you for what you were, and resents you for what you are trying to become." Stokely Carmichael declares:

Integration . . . speaks to the problem of blackness in a despicable way. As a goal it has been based on complete acceptance of the fact [sic] that in order to have a decent house or education, blacks must move into a white neighborhood or send their children to a white school.

This reinforces, among both black and white, the idea that "white" is automatically better and "black" is by definition inferior. This is why integration is a subterfuge for the maintenance of white supremacy.[18]

To the black masses, the Negro integrationists and integrationist leaders take on the characteristics of "collaborators with the enemy" and need to be labeled distinctly as such. Hence, the black militants have resurrected the connotation of "Negro" as being a thing, a puppet, a creation of the white man, finding it peculiarly applicable to the Negro middle class and its leadership.[19]

Like the Garveyites and the Black Muslims before them, the new black militants—particularly those in the Student Nonviolent Coordinating Committee—do not see themselves in the image of the white American. They dress unaffectedly and wear their hair *à la mode Africaine*—combed, but unstraightened. They refer to themselves and to all other non-integrationist-minded black Americans as "black people." The term is deliberately chosen as a symbol of racial polarization. It intends to imply the solidarity of the black masses, here and

18 Stokely Carmichael, "What We Want," *The Boston Sunday Herald*, October 2, 1966.
19 In conversation, the word may be sarcastically pronounced with excessive stress on the first syllable ("NEE-gro"), recalling readily to the in-group mind the slurred pronunciation of some Southerners that renders the word "Negra," which to sensitive ears is a covert way of saying "nigger."

abroad; to disavow any necessary commitment to white values or deference to the white establishment; to distinguish the masses from the integrationists; and to exploit new feelings of black nationalism and negritude that have taken hold in the Negro community since World War II. It answers, at least for the time being, all the important questions of identity and color. Many middle-class Negroes, remembering the negative stereotypes formerly associated with blackness, cannot bring themselves to speak of Negroes as "black people." Neither can many whites for that matter.[20] The stereotypes die too hard.

The new SNCC strategy aims at organizing a power base from which black people can influence decisions within the existing political arrangement without being subject to review by white monitors. Implied is a fundamental rejection of reliance upon the white man's integrity, a point to which all black nationalist groups must come by definition. The synonym for black nationalism is black ethnocentrism, and ethnocentrism always implies a suspicion of some other peoples' integrity, their values, and their truth.

In the conventional interpretation of human confrontation, belief is always preceded by doubt. Not so with the Negro in America. He believed first and has but lately learned to doubt. It is a tragedy that doubt was even necessary, since the faith he had required so little to fulfill. But America is now forever beyond the point of naïveté and innocence and is unlikely to pass that way again. The lessons that have been learned cannot be forgotten, and there are new teachers to interpret old experiences. Elijah Muhammad justifies his all-black Muslim

[20] In a graduate seminar on minority relations, a young white student protested to a Negro classmate: "Why do you call yourself 'black'? I could never call you black. There is something not right about it. Besides, I think you're a nice guy." "You can't call me 'black,'" the Negro student answered, "and that is your guilt. I can call myself 'black,' and that is my freedom."

organization on the grounds that "You can't whip a man when he's helping you," thus surreptitiously but unequivocably identifying the enemy as the white man. The SNCC rationale is more adroit. SNCC wants its white supporters to work among prejudiced whites "who are not accessible" to its Negro agents. The net result is the same: the effective removal of white individuals, however well-intentioned, from sensitive strategy and policy-making areas where racial loyalties may jeopardize the pursuit of the black man's program.

Traditional black nationalism has been oriented toward separatism—or, at best, toward a pluralistic society. The "black-power" syndrome recognizes the substantial existence of a plural society already and intends to capitalize on it. Like the integrationists, SNCC wants power within the existing political structure, but unlike more moderate organizations, SNCC is impatient with indirect power and suspicious of contingent or shared power. "Black power" is conceived as palpable, manipulatable, black-controlled power that carries with it a sense of dignity for black people and a feeling of security from white caprice. An organized, voting black minority with a substantially unified ideological orientation could conceivably produce such power. Whether it can be produced on the basis of color alone is debatable.[21]

The question is not whether black people are capable of leadership and self-direction or of making the sacrifices that may be needed. They have demonstrated their capabilities in all these areas and more. The more fundamental question is whether color alone is a unifying force sufficient to weld together in a monolithic (or, better, monochromatic) socio-

[21] Malcolm X saw color as the only possible basis of unification. He attempted to eclipse the problem of white ancestry so obvious in many Negroes, himself included, by declaring: "We are all black, different shades of black, and not one of us means any more to a white cracker than any other one."

political movement a black minority exhibiting an immense spectrum of needs, wants, desires, and intentions based on conflicting systems of value. The question of identity has not been resolved. Color alone does not answer satisfactorily the questions about the self one needs to have answered as the basis for intelligent decision-making about himself and others. Negroes in America still do not know who they are. Not having resolved this elemental problem, they approach all other problems in human relations with predictable ambivalence and uncertainty. That is why they fight bravely in the far-off places of the world, march peacefully in Washington, and die cravenly in Mississippi and Alabama. This, too, is why they sing "Black and White Together" by day, and "Burn! Baby, Burn!" by night.

The Negro's experiences in America have produced in him a mass social neurosis that can only become more morbid as the frustrations of trying to cope with the problem of color and identity are intensified by education and increased marginality at the top of the social pyramid, and by increasing poverty and the concomitant loss of personhood at the bottom. Involuntary servitude did not shatter the psyche of the Negro. He could overcome servitude—slavery if you insist—just as countless other peoples of indifferent races and cultures had. Slavery was not a unique experience; nowhere but in America was it accompanied by such devastation of personality. It was not the slavery per se, but the pitiless obliteration of the history and the culture of a people, the deliberate distortion of that history and culture. It was the casual pollution of a race without the compassion and responsibility of acknowledgment. It was, above all, the snide rejection of the Negro's claim to be "American." Less deserving people from all over the world could come to America and claim that identity so long as they were white. The Negro could never claim it because he was black.

The trauma of this rejection polarizes the color crisis between the races and keeps alive the anxieties of identification
and color within the Negro subgroup. Charles Silberman is
probably right: "Consciousness of color is not likely to disappear unless color itself disappears, or unless men lose their
eyesight." [22] But consciousness of color, like consciousness of
kind, is not a reasonable basis upon which to project a system
of intergroup relations. Nor has it ever been.

[22] Charles E. Silberman, *Crisis in Black and White* (New York: Random
House, 1964), p. 166.

THE BLACK GHETTO AS
AN URBAN PHENOMENON

The black ghetto is the enduring visible symbol of racial apartheid in America. It countermands the message of all the gaunt, tired churches whose congregations have departed to suburbia and ensconced themselves behind new palisades of racial virtue. Its persistence calls into question the democratic suppositions upon which this republic was founded and vitiates the image of "the good life in America" we like to flaunt before the natives abroad. But above all, and infinitely more fundamental to our corporate well-being today *and* tomorrow, the black ghetto represents the increasing polarization between a large black minority and a white majority in this country with unpredictable social and political consequences. The *black ghetto* points to, and is part of, an American problem of the first magnitude. Neither the Red Russians nor the Yellow Chinese are potentially as dangerous to the national integrity as is the forced maintenance of the black ghetto in the central cities of the United States.

"Individuals who enjoy the highest status also enjoy premium positions in space."[1] This might well be called a first

[1] James W. Vander Zanden, *Sociology* (New York: Ronald Press, 1965), p. 464.

principle of human ecology. The principle is applied rigidly in
the segregation of individuals by race (and race is an essential
condition for high status) here in America. The white Anglo-
Saxon Protestant is still the ideal type, and the emphasis remains on "white." Not long ago, in some parts of this country,
race determined where one sat on the bus, which rest rooms
and what hotels, if any, were available. Today, in *all* parts of
the country, race still determines where one may normally
buy a house, go to school, or worship God. As an ecological
principle, status is still the key to desirable spaces, and race is
the key to admission to the lists of mobility where the prize
of status may be pursued. The Negro cannot compete because
he cannot even get in the lists. Race is the bar to the tourna-
ment.

The deteriorated "central city" is a traditional characteristic
of the transitional nature of the urban evolutionary process.
The black ghetto, which now characterizes the central city in
most urban areas, is a unique phenomenon which embarrasses
the social theories of an earlier generation and defies the most
carefully programmed contemporary sociological techniques
aimed at solution. Gunnar Myrdal says that the assimilation of
her minorities is part of the value creed of the United States,
but it is to be understood, says Myrdal, that racial minorities
are excluded.[2] They do not melt in the great American melting pot.

A generation ago Professors Robert E. Park and Ernest W.
Burgess, at the University of Chicago, developed the concentric circle theory which conceived the modern city as a pattern of contiguous, concentric zones beginning with a central
core or hub, and radiating outward like waves defining the

[2] George E. Simpson and J. Milton Yinger, *Racial and Cultural Minorities*
(3rd ed.; New York: Harper and Row, 1965), p. 21.

point of impact of a pebble in a pool of water.[3] Each circle
or zone has its own distinguishing characteristics; Zone One,
"the hub," is the central business district. Hard by is Zone
Two, which begins somewhere in the limbo between the
reputable business houses and the cheap men's hotels, wine-
shops, pawnshops, and ethnic groceries.

Zone Two is the zone of transition. The once elegant mansions of the rich, long since fled to newer and more exclusive
elegances, have become the rooming houses of the poor. A
class of *invaders* has become successors to a class of *evaders*.
Zone Two is the "central city." Today it is likely to be the
heart of the black ghetto. Beyond it lies Zone Three, representing the (white) working class, and beyond that increasingly more desirable residential areas until one reaches the
Commuter's Zone, that Elysium of middle-class America
called "suburbia."

There are other theories of the internal structure of cities,
of course,[4] none of which fit precisely the ecological configu-
rations of race space, but the concentric conceptualization is
a useful tool for examining the history and the structure of the
black ghetto. It is frequently argued that Negroes who live in
the deteriorated central city are simply following a pattern set
by white immigrant groups who were there before them—the
Irish, the Jews, the Italians, the Poles, and others, and that the
travail of the central city is the certain and necessary condition of assimilation. Even when such a suggestion is made with
sincerity, the viciousness of its naïveté can hardly be over-
stated. The relative sociological, psychological, and historical

[3] See Robert E. Park, Ernest W. Burgess, and R. D. McKenzie, *The City*
(Chicago: University of Chicago Press, 1925).
[4] See, for example, Chauncy D. Harris and Edward R. Ullman, "The Nature
of Cities," *The Annals of the American Academy of Political and Social
Sciences*, November, 1945, p. 242.

factors are enormously dissimilar, and on the basis of the white man's response to the black man's most recent efforts to be assimilated into the American mainstream, there is little indication that the Irish and the Poles or the Jews set a pattern that the Negro can follow beyond the gates of the ghetto. In the first place, obviously, it would have been impossible to maintain the strict segregation of white ethnic groups even had it been desired. Secondly, in every case the segregation of white immigrant groups, which was never more than nominal, has always declined with the passage of time.

Contemporary studies show uniformly that the segregation of Negroes in the central cities of America is steadily increasing.[5] Louis Wirth's celebrated studies of the immigrant ghettos in Chicago noted that a chief functional characteristic of the American ghetto was to provide "ways in which cultural groups [could] give expression to their heritages when transplanted to a strange habitat." This function could scarcely appeal to the Negro whose cultural heritage is one with that of the oldest American. Nor could America for him be in any sense a "strange habitat." Although Professor Wirth falls into the common error of assuming that "The Negro has drifted into the abandoned sections of the ghetto for precisely [*sic*] the same reasons that the Jews and the Italians came there," he fails to go the next logical step to see why Negroes remain when all others are gone. He writes:

> It is the children of the immigrant who discover the ghetto and then . . . flee. What a few years ago was a steady but slow outward movement has now developed into a veritable stampede to get out of the ghetto; for with all its varied ac-

5 See Otis Dudley Duncan and Stanley Lieberson, "Ethnic Segregation and Assimilation," *American Journal of Sociology*, Vol. 64, January, 1959. See also Stanley Lieberson, *Ethnic Patterns in American Cities* (Glencoe, Ill.: Free Press, 1963); and Karl and Alma Taeuber, *Negroes in Cities— Residential Segregation and Neighborhood Change* (Chicago: Aldine, 1965).

tivities, and its colorful atmosphere, *the ghetto nevertheless is a small world. It throbs with a life which is provincial and sectarian. Its successes are measured on a small scale, and its range of expression is limited: Not until the immigrant leaves the ghetto does he become fully conscious of himself and his status. He feels a sense* of personal freedom. . . . [Italics mine.] [6]

The children of the Negro do not flee from the ghetto. They can't. They are hemmed in on every side by high, white walls of prejudice which keep them back from the life-giving air of freedom and the fullness of self-expression. So the world of the Negro *must* be small. If one cannot become "conscious of himself and his status . . . cannot feel a sense of personal freedom" so long as he is in the ghetto, then that is the common lot of the black man in America.

There are approximately 22 million Negroes in the United States today, and most of them live in cities. This was not always the case, for the primary purpose of the Negro's being here in the first place was that his labor could be exploited in the cultivation of cotton, cane, and indigo on the vast plantations of the South. The characteristic experience of the Negro in America was that of a rural-dwelling, agricultural worker. At the time of the first census in 1790, 91 per cent of the Negroes lived in the South,[7] a ratio which had changed only 2 percentage points (to 89 per cent) 120 years later in 1910. By contrast, according to the 1960 census, of the 20,491,000 Americans listed as "nonwhite," almost three-fourths of them lived in cities, and more than half of them lived outside the South.[8]

[6] Louis Wirth, "The Ghetto," *American Journal of Sociology*, Vol. 33, July, 1927.

[7] Most of the demographic information below is taken from Philip M. Hauser, "Demographic Factors," *Daedalus*, Fall, 1965.

[8] August Meier and Elliot Rudwick, *From Plantation to Ghetto* (New York: Hill and Wang, 1966), p. 189.

The Negro movement away from the farms and plantations actually began during and after the Civil War. Since their liberators came from "the North," and since the North had traditionally been a land of refuge and a major terminus for the Underground Railroad, a substantial number of ex-slaves made their way to the Northern metropolises. Others trudged toward the cities of the South. In both cases bitter disappointment awaited most of them.

Whereas a good deal of humanitarian idealism has been a part of the motivation that set white America against itself, that idealism—like that of the civil rights movement a hundred years later—did not survive the activistic phase represented by the invasion of the South. Negroes who expected to be welcomed in the North by the very people who had put themselves to such an inconvenience to destroy slavery in the South were disillusioned by the indifference and the undisguised hostility they encountered in the Northern cities. Northern idealism quickly shifted on to other causes, and Northern humanitarianism reasoned that since the Negro was "free," the rest was up to him. He could pull himself up from freedom by his own bootstraps—preferably down South where he belonged. The North was preoccupied with exploiting the industrial boom generated by the war, and the Negro migrant from the Southern plantations had few skills and no capital to recommend him to the prevailing interests. An endless labor supply now streamed in from Europe: men with technical skills; men with centuries-old crafts; men who were relatives from the old country—who preempted the jobs, the housing that otherwise might have gone to the new black citizens of America.

On the other hand, many of the cities of the Old South were built by a talented class of Negro artisans, both freemen and slaves who were hired out by the month or by the year. The intricate ironwork of the French Quarter in New Orleans, the old courthouses of Jackson, Mississippi, and Montgomery, Alabama, the grand mansions of Vicksburg, Holly Springs, and Charleston remain no less as monuments to the artistry and technical skill of the Negro than of the romantic mysticism of a departed era. But after the war, the Negro artisans then in the cities were assiduously pushed out of their traditional jobs by a new class of impoverished whites created by the war, and Negroes coming in from the plantations found their prospects for survival unencouraging.

Rebuffed by the social and economic realities prevailing in the cities of the North and the South immediately following the Civil War, the Negro turned back to the plantation. There as the working partner of the Northern banker and the Southern landowner, he became a sharecropper, pledging his loyalty to the white man and his labor to the land for the generations he still needed to make freedom meaningful. From time to time small groups seeking the relative independence of renters and ownership left the worn-out lands of the old cotton culture and pushed westward into the as yet undeveloped regions of Georgia, Alabama, the lush Mississippi Delta, and even beyond into Arkansas and Louisiana and Texas. They were not to find freedom there, nor yet economic independence, for it would turn out that the very counties to which they turned for a new start and a new life as free and productive Americans would forthwith distinguish themselves by their devotion to the lynch rope and the flaming cross, and by a crass interpretation of white supremacy as meaning total black subjection in every single aspect of racial contact or style of life.

By the turn of the century a certain restlessness had begun to stir America, and while spatial mobility could hardly be said to be characteristic of the general population, Americans were on the move and have been ever since. In 1910, 77 per cent of the white population lived in the same state where they were born. Negroes were considerably more cautious then about leaving home—93 per cent of *them* lived in the same states where they were born. Yet, by 1911, the trickle of Negroes to the great cities of the North was sufficient to justify the establishment in New York of the National League on Urban Conditions among Negroes (The National Urban League), which reported that "the migration of Negroes to the cities . . . is a fact of common observation." Today, in a society characterized by mobility, the migratory habits of Negroes slightly exceed those of whites. The last hard data available show that in 1960 only 64 per cent of the Negroes still lived in the states where they were born as compared with 68 per cent of the whites.

Most of the movement of Negroes has been toward the large cities of the North and West. Professor Philip M. Hauser of the University of Chicago estimates that "six states in the North and West (California, Illinois, Michigan, New York, Ohio, and Pennsylvania) absorbed 72 per cent of all Negro net in-migration between 1910 and 1950," and that "between 1950 and 1960 the same six states absorbed 68 per cent of all net in-migration of nonwhites." [9] In fifty years the Negro has made the transition from a rural to an urban dweller, with whatever social, political, and economic implications there may be implicit in that fact. Like the American Jew, he now belongs to the metropolis. In 1910, according to Professor Hauser, "73 per cent of the Negroes in the nation, as compared with 52 per cent of the whites, lived in rural areas. . . . By 1960 the distribution . . . had become completely reversed, with 73 per cent of the Negro population residing in urban areas. . . . Negroes were more highly urbanized than whites, 70 per cent of whom resided in urban areas." [10]

How did it all happen? And why? The trickle North that

[9] Hauser, *op. cit.*, p. 851.
[10] *Ibid.*

began around the turn of the century became a veritable deluge by the end of World War I. It has continued without serious abatement except for the years of the Depression. Between 1910 and 1920 net migration of Negroes from the South was 454,000; between 1920 and 1930, about three-quarters of a million; from 1930 to 1940, 347,000; during the next decennium between 1940 and 1950, 1.2 million, and between 1950 and 1960, 1.5 million. As in most large-scale migrations, there were extraordinary factors of attraction, or "pull" and complementing factors of expulsion, or "push," which provided impetus to the hegira. The pull *and* the push were in this case social and economic. The Negro had never lost faith in the promise that he could be a full participant in the American Dream. Perhaps if not in the South, then certainly in the North. Somewhere within the vast reaches of this democratic commonwealth there was a place for the black man to realize the fullness of the freedom the law declared to be his. This was the pull. The Negro had despaired of finding freedom in the South—political or economic.

In the South the total abrogation of the black man's rights was symbolized by the common practice of the savage custom of lynching, and by the social acceptance of the practice as a desirable methodology for "keeping the nigger in his place," and by the indisposition of any government, local, state, or federal, to do anything effective about it. In the last sixteen years of the nineteenth century, 2,500 human beings were sacrificed to the rope and faggot. Thereafter, from 1900 to the outbreak of World War I in 1914, the pace of the killings was more leisurely; an annual average of seventy-eight black men and women graced the magnolias, or popped and sputtered in the bonfires before the altar of white supremacy.[11] This was the big push.

[11] John Hope Franklin, *From Slavery to Freedom* (New York: Alfred A. Knopf, 1956), pp. 431–32.

There were other factors: Many Negro sharecroppers had
been reduced to peonage through the connivance of local
sheriffs and unscrupulous landowners. A chief feature of the
sharecropper arrangement was the "furnishing" of the Negro's family with food—traditionally salt pork, corn meal, and
molasses—against his share of the crop he undertook to make.
Seed, fertilizer, and work animals were also furnished by the
white landowner (who in turn borrowed his operating capital
from the Northern bankers). If at harvest time the landowner
(who kept the books) declared that the Negro's "share" of
the crop did not cover the furnishings made to him, then the
Negro was bound to work another year until the deficit was
made up. He could not leave the land under penalty of im-
prisonment, and nowhere in the courts of the South was his
testimony accepted against that of a white man. Isolated cases
of peonage were still being litigated in the federal courts as
late as the 1950's.

Another push came from the Mexican boll weevil which
invaded the cotton lands of Texas and, moving eastward,
eventually destroyed a great part of the cotton economy of
the Old South. In 1915 there were devastating floods in Mississippi and Alabama which inundated the crops and uprooted
thousands from their homes. And too, in 1915, the Ku Klux
Klan was reorganized at Stone Mountain near Atlanta, Georgia, and the terror of that hooded order of hoodlums spread
once more across the South.

Suddenly there was plenty of pull from the great industrial
centers of the North. The World War had cut off the flow
of immigrants from Europe at precisely the time when industrial America needed all the labor it could get. There were
ships, tanks, guns and munitions to be made. Our own armies
and those of our allies overseas had to be supplied. There was
now a place for Negro labor, skilled or unskilled. Suddenly it
was discovered that Negroes could be trained for skills like

anyone else. Labor agents from the North toured the South signing up whole families and advancing them railroad fare. The Negro newspapers of the North told of the high wages, the good schooling, the freedom to be had in the Northern cities and urged their readers below the Mason and Dixon line to hurry North to the Promised Land.

Hurry they did. They stole away from the plantations at night to avoid the wrath of the white landowners. Some traveled through the swamps and thickets like hunted animals until they reached a rail station far from their native plantations. Cooks and maids washed the supper dishes and slipped off to the depot. On any given day hundreds of migrants from the lower South passed through the big rail junctions at Memphis, Birmingham, Atlanta, and Baltimore. They took with them their worldly goods stuffed in bags and boxes and paper sacks, which led to the emigration being labeled the "paper suitcase parade."

Not all of the migrants went North. The general movement was from South to North but also from rural to urban. By 1910 the Negro populaton was 27 per cent urban and at least a dozen cities had Negro populations of 40,000 or more. Some of the cities were in the South. New Orleans and Baltimore had over 80,000 Negroes each, but Washington and New York had 90,000 each, and Philadelphia had 80,000. During the same period the Negro population of Atlanta increased 45 per cent, and that of Birmingham, 215 per cent.[12] By 1960, 54.8 per cent of the population of Washington, D.C., was Negro. So it was with 23.6 per cent of the population of Chicago; 29.2 per cent of that of Detroit; 28.9 per cent of the population of Cleveland; 14.7 per cent of that of New York City; 26.7 per cent of Philadelphia's population; 35 per cent of Baltimore's. And Negroes comprised 16.8 per cent of the

12 Meier and Rudwick, *op. cit.*

population of Los Angeles.[13] These figures are now seven years old. Undoubtedly today's percentages are higher.

In every case these populations are closely restricted to the central city, the black ghettos of the cities I have named. And for every city I failed to name, there is a black ghetto to contain its black population if it has one. Why? The concept of the ghetto as being a desirable, even a proper place for blacks seems to be irretrievably imbedded deep in the American psyche. It is not dislodged by logic, by moral persausion or political expedience. The massive evidence that the black ghetto is detrimental to the well-being and reasonable development of a large minority of Americans, and that it exists as a serious threat to the peace and security of all Americans, has not impressed the white establishment. Lewis Killian, a distinguished Southern sociologist, warns that "the crisis in race relations is second in gravity only to the threat of nuclear war." [14] The intensity of the racial confrontation is sharply increased by the existence of the black ghetto. James B. Conant, former president of Harvard, declares that the ghetto "phenomenon may be compared to the piling up of inflammable material in an empty building in a city block. Potentialities for trouble," he says, "indeed possibilities for disasters are surely there." [15] We know all this, but we keep hoping the evil will resolve itself in some miraculous fashion without anyone having to admit its existence.

The President's Crime Commission reports that the ghetto is the biggest source of crime. Yet the federal government is a major partner in the maintenance of existing ghettos and the building of new ones. A manifesto issued by the National Committee against Discrimination in Housing charges that:

13 Percentage statistics supplied by the Urban League of Portland.
14 Vander Zanden, *op. cit.*, p. 3.
15 *Ibid.*

Everyday Federal money and power are used to build racial ghettos. Federal benefits are creating community patterns and conditions in the housing supply which *build in* segregation. Federal agencies allow municipalities to select sites for federally-aided low-cost housing in the areas where segregation is foreordained. F.H.A. [Federal Housing Authority] continues doing business with discriminatory builders, lenders and real estate brokers. Urban renewal and highway projects destroy integrated neighborhoods and swell the ghettos.[16]

Unless current practices are reversed, the manifesto argues, the model cities program will be used "to repeat for generations to come the cycle of ghettoization that has brought us to our present crisis." [17]

The persistence of the ghetto is already a national scandal. The prospect of new generations in the ghettos cannot be seriously entertained if for no other reason than that the Negro minority is growing faster than the ghetto can expand to accommodate it. Populations grow by only two methods: immigration, and natural increase, i.e., an excess of births over deaths. As late as 1810 the Negro population was one-fifth of the national total. Since the end of the slave trade in the early nineteenth century, the Negro population has had to depend on natural increase for growth, and although, due to continuing massive waves of white immigration from Europe, the ratio of blacks to whites had been reduced to 9.7 per cent by 1930, the Negro birth rate has been consistently above that of the white population. Professor Hauser reminds us that "between 1940 and 1960 the birth rates of both whites and nonwhites rose with the post-war baby boom. But nonwhite fertility increased by 90 per cent . . . while white fertility rose by 88 per cent." [18] And this occurred while the Negro was

[16] N.C.D.H., *Trends in Housing*, February, 1967, p. 1.
[17] *Ibid.*
[18] Hauser, *op. cit.*

making the transition from the plantation to the ghetto!

By 1960 the ratio of Negroes to whites had climbed to 10.6 per cent and was still rising. Whites still live longer than Negroes because of the considerable gap which remains in money income and the availability of medical services, proper food, and conditions of living. However, by 1960 as compared with 1900, the differences in life expectancy had been cut in half— from 14.6 years to 7.0 years.[19] The ratio is still declining. Because the mortality rate is going down and the fertility rate is going up, nonwhite natural increase was, in 1960, 22.0, or two-thirds greater than the white rate which stood at 13.2.[20] Further, the Negro population is considerably younger,[21] which leads to the reasonable conclusion that its birth rate will continue to increase and its death rate will continue to decline.

The prospects, then, are for a steadily increasing black population. It seems destined to be a ghetto population. Yet, while the ghettos of this country are extensive, even with the characteristic wretchedness of crowded living conditions, crowded schools, and absent parks and playgrounds, they will be inadequate to contain physically the projected black population. But the crucial issue has nothing to do with the problems of physical accommodation. There is an ever-present explosive potential inherent in a situation in which people are physically bottled up. The invisible walls of the black ghetto are as repressive and confining and as demeaning as those of Leavenworth or Alcatraz, and the social and political machinery which maintains them is no less final and absolute. But unlike the residents of Alcatraz, the people who live in the black ghetto are conscious of no offense against society.

[19] Hauser, *op. cit.*

[20] *Ibid.*

[21] In 1960, according to Professor Hauser, the median age of nonwhites was 23.5 and that of whites, 30.0 years respectively.

Rather, society has committed a monstrous offense against them. And they resent it. Like the people behind the Berlin Wall, they will continue to risk their lives to get out—to breathe free. In this fact alone lies the potential for disaster.

We are faced with an intolerable dilemma which, if it is not resolved, will be a sinister determinant in the direction that racial relations and politics will take in this country. The black man is more conscious than ever that he must define for himself and for all time his status and his relationships within the American commonwealth. The black ghetto is a symbol of white rejection. But it is also, or it will be, a test of the black man's endurance, his self-control, his forgiveness, his politics, his organizational ability, and his administrative potential. Suddenly America has discovered that "Other American." He is there in the heart of her great cities—in endless numbers. Yes, even in alarming numbers. But the black American has also discovered himself. He has been pushed, pulled, dragged, kicked, and self-propelled onto center stage, and now he has to act.

Before he can act he must come to terms with his situation. He does not want to be told that he is now where the Irish and the Jews used to be. He knows that is a simple answer to a complex relationship. It is no answer at all. He is merely occupying some physical space once occupied by European immigrants, and there the similarity ends. As a black American, he knows himself to be unique in the political and social history of this country. It does not lessen his problems or provide him with any particular reassurance to offer him platitudes about Irishmen and Jews. He remembers too well the lesson of Proposition Fourteen in California, when after a hundred years of the most earnest bootstrapping the people of California took a vote to see *if* he were yet fit to live among them. Nobody knows what kind of looking-glass Californians use to conjure up their own self-images, but with all the self-

righteous bigotry they could muster, they turned in an overwhelming vote at the polls to confine the black man to the
black ghetto as if he were the black plague rather than another
Californian in a nonwhite skin.

This was the prelude to the predictable failure of the
Eighty-ninth Congress to pass an open-housing bill. Whereas
the people of California were blatant and quite blunt about
the matter, the national Congress could afford to be both coy
and dilatory. The net results were the same: the black ghetto
persists—in California and throughout the nation.

The black man in the ghetto is not unaware of the implications of his confinement. Unlike his posture during the Era of
the Grand Illusion when he thought that to be free meant to
have freedom, the Negro in the ghetto has learned a certain
sophistication about the limitations of freedom, the definition
of citizenship, and the qualifications of justice. He did not
learn these truths vicariously. He learned them experientially.
He has learned, too, how far a multitude of those who wish
him well will walk with him, and how far along the lonely
road to freedom he must expect to walk by himself. The revelation of the real is the genesis of a new departure. All the
years before, all the decades and the generations that came to
be and slipped silently into the past, the Negro in America
thought he belonged—not *to* America, but *in* America and
with America.

His epic pilgrimage from Little Rock and Oxford, from
New Orleans and Birmingham, from Jackson and Selma to
Los Angeles and Boston, to Detroit and Chicago showed how
earnestly he was committed to the idea that somewhere here
in America he belonged. Nineteen sixty-six *could* have been
the year of jubilee—the fulfillment of the *black* American's
dream. Instead, the dissolution of the civil rights movement,
the defection of the white liberals, the back lash, the front
lash, and the side lash all combined with the Eighty-ninth

Congress to spell out to any who cared that the so-called pilgrimage may well have been no more than a tragic exercise in futility. At the end of the march, beyond all heroics and oblivious to all suffering, was the black ghetto—waiting.

The Negro can survive in the ghetto. He survived slavery in America, which was infinitely less humane than anywhere else in the New World. But the question is not whether he can survive, but rather whether the subculture he will build there will have compatible interests to those of the society which has excluded him. He tried to belong. Now having tasted the bitterness of rejection, he is at best ambivalent. He may no longer *want* to belong. The Adam Clayton Powell affair is hardly more a symbol of white rejection than it is of black counter-rejection. The black man's interest in integration has never been more perfunctory than it is now. His emphases, which were once largely spiritual and ideological, have shifted to the material and political benefits of his still unresolved citizenship. There is a growing consensus that schools in the ghetto should be good, not necessarily integrated, that teachers and administrators should be black, and that the curriculum should reflect the black man's history and point of view.

In the face of the realities of the growing apartheid in American life, these new lines of thinking seem reasonable. In order to preserve his psychological and political integrity, the black man now opts for new forms of social adjustment consistent with his interpretation of a new reality. If the black ghetto is to represent the area of social and political life delimiting his participation in the national expresss, the development of an increasingly distinct subculture in the midst of the prevailing order is sure and certain. Such a subculture may not necessarily be more hostile in its approach to the larger society, but it will inevitably be less accommodating, and a decisive change in its patterns of response (such as are already

recognizable) may well be *interpreted* as overt hostility, especially where feelings of guilt may be involved. If the ghetto
remains, we shall inevitably witness a phenomenon which
does critical violence to the expectations we have come to
have about the assimilation of minority groups. We shall see
the evolution of a folk society into an urban configuration,
which, while it strives for the approval and acceptance, does
not produce an assimilable fallout in its subsequent generations. Instead of the progressive divestiture of ethnic patterns
in favor of the adoption of ways of behavior approved by the
larger society, there will be a progressive intensification of
ethnic values which increases the contrast between the larger
society and the new society now a-building in the black
ghetto. As the opportunity for emotional and social reciprocal
interaction between blacks and whites diminishes, rejection
and counter-rejection will be intensified. Assimilation will be
mutually undesirable. There will develop instead a new, sub-
autonomous sub-society preoccupied with its own values and
culture symbols—its own heroes, its own myths, its own interpretations of history, and its own sense of destiny. This
black society will be nurtured by a chauvinistic nationalism
based on color—*mutatis mutandis*, the white nationalism which
created the conditions for its existence. The points of contact
between this black society in the ghetto and the encircling
white society will be formal and ritualized and will tend to
be increasingly restricted to such necessary intercourse as develops from political or economic interests. Inevitably, a color
nationalism must look beyond itself for spiritual and cultural
reinforcement. And to the degree that it finds identification
and authentication abroad, it becomes less solicitous of understanding or acceptance at home. American white nationalism is a case in point. The black nationalism spawning in the
ghetto seems destined to follow a well-defined path.

A LAST ADMONITION*

The notion of a "last lecture" makes me feel a little like Socrates must have felt as he sat in his cell waiting for the ship to arrive from Delos which would be the signal for his execution. The difference between Socrates and myself is that his body was imprisoned, but his mind was free, while my body is free and my mind is shackled with the responsibility of being at least pertinent if I cannot be profound. But Socrates and I have at least this in common: he knew and I know that the clearest and the most enduring message to be left to posterity, the best last lecture, consists not in choice words or ringing phrases or noble sentiments, but in the unadorned record of one's life. Socrates at seventy had lived a full and useful life, studded with wisdom and jeweled with integrity. He was about to leave behind him a record which would endure through the ages, illuminating countless generations, even as he had illuminated the youth of Athens while he still lived.

What can I say to you that will be meaningful enough to illuminate your lives even for an instant? Certainly I am no Socrates; and though I have accumulated some years, I do not lay claim to very much wisdom, and neither of us would be content with platitudes.

As I look at your young faces and think within myself of

* Condensed from a lecture delivered at Portland State College as one of the "Last Lecture Series" sponsored by the Koinonia House. Published in *Faculty Forum*, March, 1967.

the terrors bequeathed to you by the generations just before you, and as I search for a phrase to sum up my advice to you, my thoughts keep focusing on a single word: RUN! RUN! *RUN!*

And yet I know I would scarcely be satisfied in giving an advice that is both enigmatic and worthless, and one which is unworthy of the character and determination I see when I look at you. Yes, it is my emotions, not my reason, which want you to *run while you may!* For my emotions are sated with the stench of flesh, the sight of blood, the sound of screaming. My mind is scarred with the memories of Dachau and Buchenwald, and Hiroshima and Sharpsburg, and Little Rock, Arkansas, and Oxford, Mississippi, and Selma, Alabama.

It is my mind, not my reason. The acrid, brittle words of T. S. Eliot come to mind, and when I think of my generation and the one before, I hear his reminder that—

> We are the hollow men
> We are the stuffed men
> Leaning together
> Headpiece filled with straw. Alas! [1]

Run? Where is there to run? "Cry? What shall I cry?" "The saints and martyrs wait for those who shall be saints and martyrs."

It is only my emotions that say run. My reason knows that man must live in this world until he knows some world that is better. And my faith insists that the heritage you pass on to your children will be less contingent and less tentative than the heritage you yourselves have already received.

When I think of your heritage, and that of all America, my

---

[1] From "We Are the Hollow Men," in *Collected Poems 1909–1962* by T. S. Eliot, copyright, 1936, by Harcourt, Brace & World, Inc.; copyright, © 1963, 1964, by T. S. Eliot. Reprinted by permission of the publishers.

mind goes back to a brilliant Monday almost thirteen years ago. It was the day America redeemed itself—almost. Some of you have never known, and some of you have simply not thought much about it, and some of you have forgotten, but that day, May seventeenth, is the thirteenth anniversary of that historic Monday when the Supreme Court of the United States in the case of Brown Versus Board of Education voided forever the legal basis of the insidious dehumanizing practice of racial segregation, and in so doing restored an element of justice to American jurisprudence and a measure of dignity to the American people. It will soon be May seventeenth again. The tragedy is that thirteen years ago was already late, late in the game for the legal recognition of such elemental human rights. It was late because Buchenwald and Hiroshima had already happened, and Little Rock and Selma could not be avoided. The greater tragedy is that we are still so far from the fulfillment of the redemptive promise we held aloft that day.

For three hundred years here in America we had learned to live with the brutalization of the human spirit as an everyday aspect of our democratic experience and as an efficient cause in the machinery of our economics. For a hundred of those years we have lived with, promulgated, supported, and defended a hypocrisy so vile and so repulsive as to embarrass us even in those parts of the world where there is no pretense of religious values or political freedom. We taught our hypocrisy to our children, that is to say to *you*, and passed on to you the neurotic anxiety and the madness which keeps us embroiled in trouble and hatred at home and abroad.

What can I say to you that will undo one tangled skein of the madness that is your heritage? That will erase one line of the bitter message an inexorable finger has written on the signposts of your life? I tremble for my country, even as I do for you and for myself. There is another matter related to the first: I have a young brother who will soon take ship for Vietnam. I have a son who grows taller every day—whose shoulders broaden and toughen a little with every game of sandlot ball. And inexorably the clock ticks and the days go by, and the pages of the calendar are turned and I am nauseated with the feeling that I am preparing him for his death in some far-off jungle whose name I can't pronounce and whose people I do not know, either to love or to hate. I have a dread sense of guilt that I am educating him, and building his strength, and fattening him, as it were, to present as a human sacrifice to some brass-mawed Moloch who cannot sense the tender youth of his victims or share their desperate yearnings to be alive and free and equal. I know somehow that this Moloch is a false god, a *no*-god, and that he has other names like Bigotry and Race Hatred and that he rules in other places like Johannesburg and Mozambique.

And then in an introspective moment I have to ask myself, "Do you begrudge your country the strength needed to protect itself? To protect the *larger* interests that transcend its broken covenant with you? Do you begrudge America her survival, even though she needs *your* son? Your *black, unequal* son?" And from within me I hear myself scream a hasty and guilty denial: "NO! NO!" I remember again Socrates' argument in Plato's *Apology*, I think it is, where he reminds those who urge him to escape that he owes an obligation to the city which reared him and educated him to obey its laws, even though those laws may be unjust. In accepting the nurture and protection of the state, he felt morally bound to accept its requirements. So, too, I felt my only response must be: "When the sacrifice is to be made, take my son, too, with all the sons of all the faithful." (And I know I meant to say "patriotic" instead of "faithful.") "But better still," I prayed silently, "take me first, for I wore your colors and bore your arms before in a war to guarantee to the world Four Freedoms I can't remember."

And then there descends upon me a certain sadness as I remember that Sunday afternoon on December 7, 1941. After we had heard the radio accounts of the Japanese attack on Pearl Harbor, six of my young friends and I left the Thirty-eighth Street Y in Chicago to go downtown to the Naval Recruiting Station to volunteer to serve our country in time of war. We were rejected summarily by the officer in charge who told us with icy candor that the Navy was not accepting any nigger volunteers. But one boy from Louisiana, whose skin was fair, succeeded in passing himself off as white and went happily through the lines to take his place beside those favored Americans who were not too black to fight. That day, for the only time in my life, I wished that I could have been white—not all the way, but just enough to bear arms for my country.

Today it is different. Negroes make up 11 per cent of the population, but up to 30 per cent of the men fighting in the elite units of the American Army in Vietnam are Negroes. Their record of valor in this televised conflict provides a final corrective for a low and vicious tradition, which in all previous wars accepted black blood in the defense of this country, but could not admit that black men could be heroic. And their presence there in such large numbers is an open indictment of the grisliness of the society back home which rejected them as workers and citizens, but found for them a place of scarlet honor in the jungles of Asia.

I know a certain sadness, but my sadness is not for myself, it is for my country. We have sown to the wind and there is a wild wind we have still to reap. We have been called a nation of sheep. I know us to be a nation of Birchers and Ku Kluxers and Black Muslims and Neo-Nazis and pseudoreligionists of various stripes all avidly and selfishly competing

for minds and allegiances at a time when our survival is at
stake and when we need more than anything a reaffirmation
of support for whatever common values we still possess which
can be shared without being diminished.

And you—what have I to say to you? You must forgive me
for repeatedly straying from the matter at hand. But it is a
hard subject, and my thoughts ramble.

To you whose lives are a-building, you whose heritage the
world is, *build* in spite of the madness of yesterday or the uncertainty of tomorrow. Have the faith to build against all the
signs and premonitions of futility. If you despair, the world is
lost.

You will have distractors. *Build on.* When they ridicule
your efforts, never mind. When they laugh at your failures,
build again. When they belittle your accomplishments, smile.
The world is full of noisy, clamorous critics.

There are people in this world who are thieves of character,
thieves of ambition, thieves of reputation, and thieves of time.
Don't let them steal from you. They toil not; they reap not.
And of the worthwhile things in this world, they have not.
Their one goal in life is to have plenty of company doing
nothing. Their chief target will be you.

BUILD THE MANSION OF YOUR LIFE

Build it on a foundation that will endure. Beware of the
sands that shift with the passing winds and the changing tides.
Dig through the superficialities of conformity—yes, even the
banal conformity of the organized cult of nonconformity.
Cut down to the bedrock of the good and the true. Dare to
be profound. Dare to be intelligent. Dare to be moral; and
dare to be proud of it.

BUILD THE MANSION OF YOUR LIFE

Build it with strong beams of character and wide windows of understanding. Let love be the jewel that occupies the chief shrine. Let the light of your love shine with such a compelling beauty that friends and strangers alike will turn toward your beacon with assurance and confidence. Even in a blasé world of squares and other non-hippies, love cannot be passé: it *must* not be passé.

Conquer your fears about race. If you do not, they will conquer you. Be proud of your race; but be more proud of being human. Do not make of race a shibboleth. America is a nation of races, but *one* people.

Build gloriously. Build with successive successes, but do not be afraid of failure. There was a man whose name was Socrates who gave his life to illustrate a single moral principle. But the mansion he built in so doing has endured the better part of three thousand years.

There was a man whose name was Jesus who suffered the indescribable frustrations of being misunderstood, held in suspicion and hated by those whom he loved more than he loved his own life. In the end, he too accepted death—brutal and insulting. He died to illustrate the principle of love and to give it content and meaning.

> Let the mansion you build be tall,
> Let your mansion be spacious and wide,
> Hang your trophies from every wall,
> But let love be at home inside.

Nothing else can make your life worthwhile.

INDEX